Paris

And

Holland

Jacques Casanova de Seingalt

[ZHINGOORA BOOKS]

This digital edition is published by Zhingoora Books.

The Cover is Designed by Pallav Sethiya.

PARIS AND HOLLAND

CHAPTER I

Count Tiretta of Trevisa Abbe Coste—Lambertini, the Pope's Niece
Her Nick—Name for Tiretta The Aunt and Niece—Our Talk by
the Fireside—Punishment of Damien—Tiretta's Mistake Anger of
Madame***—Their Reconciliation—My Happiness with Mdlle.
de la Meure Silvia's Daughter—Mdlle, de la Meure Marries My
Despair and Jealousy—A Change far the Better

In the beginning of March, 1757, I received a letter from my
friend Madame Manzoni, which she sent to me by a young man
of good appearance, with a frank and high-born air, whom I
recognized as a Venetian by his accent. He was young Count
Tiretta de Trevisa, recommended to my care by Madame
Manzoni, who said that he would tell me his story, which I might
be sure would be a true one. The kind woman sent to me by him a
small box in which she told me I should find all my manuscripts,
as she did not think she would ever see me again.

I gave Tiretta the heartiest of welcomes, telling him that he could
not have found a better way to my favour than through a woman
to whom I was under the greatest obligations.

"And now, that you may be at your ease with me, I should like to
know in what manner I can be of service to you?"

"I have need of your friendship, perhaps of your purse, but at any
rate of your protection."

"You have my friendship and my protection already, and my purse is at your service."

After expressing his gratitude to me, Tiretta said,

"A year ago the Supreme Council of my country entrusted me with an employment dangerous to one of my years. I was made, with some other young gentlemen of my own age, a keeper of the Mont de Piete. The pleasures of the carnival having put us to a good deal of expense, we were short of money, and borrowed from the till hoping to be able to make up the money before balancing-day, but hoping all in vain.

"The fathers of my two companions, richer than mine, paid the sums they had taken, and I, not being able to pay, took the part of escaping by flight from the shame and the punishment I should have undergone.

"Madame Manzoni advised me to throw myself on your mercy, and she gave me a little box which you shall have to-day. I only got to Paris yesterday, and have only two louis, a little linen, and the clothes on my back. I am twenty-five, have an iron constitution, and a determination to do all in my power to make an honest living; but I can do nothing. I have not cultivated any one talent in a manner to make use of it now. I can play on the flute, but only as an amateur. I only know my own language, and I have no taste for literature. So what can you make of me? I must add that I have not a single expectation, least of all from my father, for to save the honour of the family he will be obliged to sell

4

my portion of the estate, to which I shall have to bid an eternal farewell."

If the count's story had surprised me, the simplicity with which he told it had given me pleasure; and I was resolved to do honour to Madame Manzoni's introduction, feeling that it was my duty to serve a fellow-countryman, who was really guilty of nothing worse than gross thoughtlessness.

"Begin," said I, "by bringing your small belongings to the room next to mine, and get your meals there. I will pay for everything while I am looking out for something which may do for you.

"We will talk of business to-morrow, for as I never dine here I rarely if ever come home till late, and I do not expect to have the honour of seeing you again today. Leave me for the present, as I have got some work to do; and if you go out to walk, beware of bad company, and whatever you do keep your own counsel. You are fond of gaming, I suppose?"

"I hate it, as it has been the cause of half my troubles."

"And the other half, I'll wager, was caused by women."

"You have guessed aright—oh, those women!"

"Well, don't be angry with them, but make them pay for the ill they have done you."

"I will, with the greatest pleasure, if I can."

"If you are not too particular in your goods, you will find Paris rich in such commodities."

"What do you mean by particular? I would never be a prince's pathic."

"No, no, I was not thinking of that. I mean by 'particular' a man who cannot be affectionate unless he is in love. The man who . . . ."

"I see what you mean, and I can lay no claim to such a character. Any hag with golden eyes will always find me as affectionate as a Celadon."

"Well said! I shall soon be able to arrange matters for you."

"I hope you will."

"Are you going to the ambassador's?"

"Good God!—no! What should I do when I got there? Tell him my story?
He might make things unpleasant for me."

"Not without your going to see him, but I expect he is not concerning himself with your case."

"That's all I ask him."

"Everybody, my dear count, is in mourning in Paris, so go to my tailor's and get yourself a black suit. Tell him you come from me, and say you want it by tomorrow. Good bye."

I went out soon after, and did not come back till midnight. I found the box which Madame Manzoni had sent me in my room, and in it my manuscripts and my beloved portraits, for I never pawned a snuff-box without taking the portrait out.

Next day Tiretta made his appearance all in black, and thanked me for his transformation.

"They are quick, you see, at Paris. It would have taken a week at Trevisa."

"Trevisa, my dear fellow, is not Paris."

As I said this, the Abbe de la Coste was announced. I did not know the name, but I gave orders for him to be admitted; and there presently appeared the same little priest with whom I had dined at Versailles after leaving the Abbe de la Ville.

After the customary greetings he began by complimenting me on the success of my lottery, and then remarked that I had distributed tickets for more than six thousand francs.

"Yes," I said, "and I have tickets left for several thousands more."

"Very good, then I will invest a thousand crowns in it."

"Whenever you please. If you call at my office you can choose the numbers."

"No, I don't think I'll trouble to do so; give me any numbers just as they come."

"Very good; here is the list you can choose from."

He chose numbers to the amount of three thousand francs, and then asked me for a piece of paper to write an acknowledgment.

"Why so? I can't do business that way, as I only dispose of my tickets for cash."

"But you may be certain that you will have the money to-morrow."

"I am quite sure I should, but you ought to be certain that you will have the tickets to-morrow. They are registered at my office, and I can dispose of them in no other manner."

"Give me some which are not registered."

"Impossible; I could not do it."

"Why not?"

"Because if they proved to be winning numbers I should have to pay out of my own pocket an honour I do not desire."

"Well, I think you might run the risk."

"I think not, if I wish to remain an honest man, at all events."

The abbe, who saw he could get nothing out of me, turned to Tiretta, and began to speak to him in bad Italian, and at last offered to introduce him to Madame de Lambertini, the widow of one of the Pope's nephews. Her name, her relationship to the Pope, and the abbe's spontaneous offer, made me curious to know more, so I said that my friend would accept his offer, and that I would have the honour to be of the party; whereupon we set out.

We got down at the door of the supposed niece of the Holy Father in the Rue Christine, and we proceeded to go upstairs. We saw a woman who, despite her youthful air, was, I am sure, not a day under forty. She was rather thin, had fine black eyes, a good complexion, lively but giddy manners, was a great laugher, and still capable of exciting a passing fancy. I soon made myself at home with her, and found out, when she began to talk, that she was neither a widow nor the niece of the Pope. She came from Modena, and was a mere adventuress. This discovery shewed me what sort of a man the abbe was.

I thought from his expression that the count had taken a fancy to her, and when she asked us to dinner I refused on the plea of an engagement; but Tiretta, who took my meaning, accepted. Soon after I went away with the abbe, whom I dropped at the Quai de la Ferraille, and I then went to beg a dinner at Calsabigi's.

After dinner Calsabigi took me on one side, and told me that M. du Vernai had commissioned him to warn me that I could not dispose of tickets on account.

"Does M. du Vernai take me for a fool or a knave? As I am neither, I shall complain to M. de Boulogne."

"You will be wrong; he merely wanted to warn you and not offend you."

"You offend me very much yourself, sir, in talking to me in that fashion; and you may make up your mind that no one shall talk to me thus a second time."

Calsabigi did all in his power to quiet me down, and at last persuaded me to go with him to M. du Vernai's. The worthy old gentleman seeing the rage I was in apologized to me for what he had said, and told me that a certain Abbe de la Coste had informed him that I did so. At this I was highly indignant, and I told him what had happened that morning, which let M. du Vernai know what kind of a man the abbe was. I never saw him again, either because he got wind of my discovery, or because a happy chance kept him out of my way; but I heard, three years after, that he had been condemned to the hulks for selling tickets of a Trevaux lottery which was non-existent, and in the hulks he died.

Next day Tiretta came in, and said he had only just returned.

"You have been sleeping out, have you, master profligate?"

"Yes, I was so charmed with the she-pope that I kept her company all the night."

"You were not afraid of being in the way?"

"On the contrary, I think she was thoroughly satisfied with my conversation."

"As far as I can see, you had to bring into play all your powers of eloquence."

"She is so well pleased with my fluency that she has begged me to accept a room in her house, and to allow her to introduce me as a cousin to M. le Noir, who, I suppose, is her lover."

"You will be a trio, then; and how do you think you will get on together?"

"That's her business. She says this gentleman will give me a good situation in the Inland Revenue."

"Have you accepted her offer?"

"I did not refuse it, but I told her that I could do nothing without your advice. She entreated me to get you to come to dinner with her on Sunday."

"I shall be happy to go."

I went with my friend, and as soon as the harebrain saw us she fell on Tiretta's neck, calling him dear Count "Six-times"—a name which stuck to him all the time he was at Paris.

"What has gained my friend so fine a title, madam?"

"His erotic achievements. He is lord of an honour of which little is known in France, and I am desirous of being the lady."

"I commend you for so noble an ambition."

After telling me of his feats with a freedom which chewed her exemption from vulgar prejudice, she informed me that she wished her cousin to live in the same house, and had already obtained M. le Noir's permission, which was given freely.

"M. le Noir," added the fair Lambertini, "will drop in after dinner, and
I am dying to introduce Count 'Sixtimes' to him."

After dinner she kept on speaking of the mighty deeds of my countryman, and began to stir him up, while he, no doubt, pleased to have a witness to his exploits, reduced her to silence. I confess that I witnessed the scene without excitement, but as I could not help seeing the athletic person of the count, I concluded that he might fare well everywhere with the ladies.

About three o'clock two elderly women arrived, to whom the Lambertini eagerly introduced Count "Six-times." In great astonishment they enquired the origin of his title, and the heroine of the story having whispered it to them, my friend became an object of interest.

"I can't believe it," said one of these ladies, ogling the count, while his face seemed to say,

"Would you like to try?"

Shortly after, a coach stopped at the door, and a fat woman of middle-aged appearance and a very pretty girl were ushered in; after them came a pale man in a black suit and a long wig. After greeting them in a manner which implied intimacy, the Pope's niece introduced her cousin Count "Six-strokes". The elderly woman seemed to be astonished at such a name, but the Lambertini gave no explanation. Nevertheless, people seemed to think it rather curious that a man who did not know a word of French should be living in Paris, and that in spite of his ignorance he continued to jabber away in an easy manner, though nobody could understand what he was talking about.

After some foolish conversation, the Pope's niece proposed a game at Loo. She asked me to play but on my refusing did not make a point of it, but she insisted on her cousin being her partner.

"He knows nothing about cards," said she; "but that's no matter, he will learn, and I will undertake to instruct him."

As the girl, by whose beauty I was struck, did not understand the game, I offered her a seat by the fire, asking her to grant me the honour of keeping her company, whereupon the elderly woman who had brought her began to laugh, and said I should have some difficulty in getting her niece to talk about anything, adding, in a polite manner, that she hoped I would be lenient with her as she had only just left a convent. I assured her that I should have no difficulty in amusing myself with one so amiable, and the game having begun I took up my position near the pretty niece.

I had been near her for several minutes, and solely occupied in mute admiration of her beauty, when she asked me who was that handsome gentleman who talked so oddly.

"He is a nobleman, and a fellow-countryman of mine, whom an affair of honour has banished from his country."

"He speaks a curious dialect."

"Yes, but the fact is that French is very little spoken in Italy; he will soon pick it up in Paris, and then he will be laughed at no longer. I am sorry to have brought him here, for in less than twenty-four hours he was spoiled."

"How spoiled?"

"I daren't tell you as, perhaps, your aunt would not like it."

"I don't think I should tell her, but, perhaps, I should not have asked."

"Oh, yes! you should; and as you wish to know I will make no mystery of it. Madame Lambertini took a fancy to him; they passed the night together, and in token of the satisfaction he gave her she has given him the ridiculous nickname of 'Count Sixtimes.' That's all. I am vexed about it, as my friend was no profligate."

Astonishment—and very reasonable astonishment—will be expressed that I dared to talk in this way to a girl fresh from a convent; but I should have been astonished myself at the bare idea of any respectable girl coming to Lambertini's house. I fixed my gaze on my fair companion, and saw the blush of shame mounting over her pretty face; but I thought that might have more than one meaning.

Judge of my surprise when, two minutes afterwards, I heard this question:

"But what has 'Sixtimes' got to do with sleeping with Madame Lambertini?"

"My dear young lady, the explanation is perfectly simple: my friend in a single night did what a husband often takes six weeks to do."

"And you think me silly enough to tell my aunt of what we have been talking? Don't believe it."

"But there's another thing I am sorry about."

"You shall tell me what that is directly."

The reason which obliged the charming niece to retire for a few minutes may be guessed without our going into explanations. When she came back she went behind her aunt's chair, her eyes fixed on Tiretta, and then came up to me, and taking her seat again, said:

"Now, what else is it that you are sorry about?" her eyes sparkling as she asked the question.

"May I tell you, do you think?"

"You have said so much already, that I don't think you need have any scruples in telling me the rest."

"Very good: you must know, then, that this very day and in my presence he—— -her."

"If that displeased you, you must be jealous."

"Possibly, but the fact is that I was humbled by a circumstance I dare not tell you."

"I think you are laughing at me with your 'dare not tell you.'"

"God forbid, mademoiselle! I will confess, then, that I was humbled because Madame Lambertini made me see that my friend was taller than myself by two inches."

"Then she imposed on you, for you are taller than your friend."

"I am not speaking of that kind of tallness, but another; you know what I mean, and there my friend is really monstrous."

"Monstrous! then what have you to be sorry about? Isn't it better not to be monstrous?"

"Certainly; but in the article we are discussing, some women, unlike you, prefer monstrosity."

"I think that's absurd of them, or rather mad; or perhaps, I have not sufficiently clear ideas on the subject to imagine what size it would be to be called monstrous; and I think it is odd that such a thing should humble you."

"You would not have thought it of me, to see me?"

"Certainly not, for when I came into the room I thought you looked a well-proportioned man, but if you are not I am sorry for you."

"I won't leave you in doubt on the subject; look for yourself, and tell me what you think."

"Why, it's you who are the monster! I declare you make me feel quite afraid."

At this she began to perspire violently, and went behind her aunt's chair. I did not stir, as I was sure she would soon come back, putting her down in my own mind as very far removed from silliness or innocence either. I supposed she wished to affect what she did not possess. I was, moreover, delighted at having taken the opportunity so well. I had punished her for having tried to impose on me; and as I had taken a great fancy to her, I was pleased that she seemed to like her punishment. As for her possession of wit, there could be no doubt on that point, for it was she who had sustained the chief part in our dialogue, and my sayings and doings were all prompted by her questions, and the persevering way in which she kept to the subject.

She had not been behind her aunt's chair for five minutes when the latter was looed. She, not knowing whom to attack, turned on her niece and said, "Get you gone, little silly, you are bringing me bad luck! Besides, it is bad manners to leave the gentleman who so kindly offered to keep you company all by himself."

The amiable niece made not answer, and came back to me smiling. "If my aunt knew," said she, "what you had done to me, she would not have accused me of bad manners."

"I can't tell you how sorry I am. I want you to have some evidence of my repentance, but all that I can do is to go. Will you be offended if I do?"

"If you leave me, my aunt will call me a dreadful stupid, and will say that I have tired you out."

"Would you like me to stay, then?"

"You can't go."

"Had you no idea what I shewed you was like till just now?"

"My ideas on the subject were inaccurate. My aunt only took me out of the convent a month ago, and I had been there since I was seven."

"How old are you now?"

"Seventeen. They tried to make me take the veil, but not having any relish for the fooleries of the cloister I refused."

"Are you vexed with me?"

"I ought to be very angry with you, but I know it was my fault, so I will only ask you to be discreet."

"Don't be afraid, if I were indiscreet I should be the first to suffer."

"You have given me a lesson which will come in useful. Stop! stop! or I will go away."

"No, keep quiet; it's done now."

I had taken her pretty hand, with which she let me do as I liked, and at last when she drew it back she was astonished to find it wanted wiping.

"What is that?"

"The most pleasant of substances, which renovates the world."

"I see you are an excellent master. Your pupils make rapid progress, and you give your lessons with such a learned air."

"Now don't be angry with me for what has happened. I should never have dared to go so far if your beauty had not inspired me."

"Am I to take that speech as a declaration of love?"

"Yes, it is bold, sweetheart, but it is sincere. If it were not, I should be unworthy both of you and of myself."

"Can I believe you?"

"Yes, with all your heart. But tell me if I may hope for your love?"

"I don't know. All I know at present is that I ought to hate you, for in the space of a quarter of an hour you have taught me what I thought I should never know till I was married."

"Are you sorry?"

"I ought to be, although I feel that I have nothing more to learn on a matter which I never dared to think about. But how is it that you have got so quiet?"

"Because we are talking reasonably and after the rapture love requires some repose. But look at this!"

"What! again? Is that the rest of the lesson?"

"It is the natural result of it."

"How is it that you don't frighten me now?"

"The soldier gets used to fire."

"I see our fire is going out."

With these words she took up a stick to poke the fire, and as she was stooping down in a favourable position my rash hand dared to approach the porch of the temple, and found the door closed in such sort that it would be necessary to break it open if one wished to enter the sanctuary. She got up in a dignified way, and told me in a polite and feeling manner that she was a well-born girl and worthy of respect. Pretending to be confused I made a thousand excuses, and I soon saw the amiable expression return to the face which it became so well. I said that in spite of my repentance I was glad to know that she had never made another man happy.

"Believe me," she said, "that if I make anyone happy it will be my husband, to whom I have given my hand and heart."

I took her hand, which she abandoned to my rapturous kisses. I had reached this pleasant stage in the proceedings when M. le Noir was announced, he having come to enquire what the Pope's niece had to say to him.

M. le Noir, a man of a certain age and of a simple appearance, begged the company to remain seated. The Lambertini introduced me to him, and he asked if I were the artist; but on being informed that I was his elder brother, he congratulated me on my lottery and the esteem in which M. du Vernai held me. But what interested him most was the cousin whom the fair niece of the Pope introduced to him under his real name of Tiretta, thinking, doubtless, that his new title would not carry much weight with M. le Noir. Taking up the discourse, I told him that the count was commanded to me by a lady whom I greatly esteemed, and that he had been obliged to leave his country for the present on account of an affair of honour. The Lambertini added that she wished to accommodate him, but had not liked to do so till she had consulted M. le Noir. "Madam," said the worthy man, "you have sovereign power in your house, and I shall be delighted to see the count in your society."

As M. le Noir spoke Italian very well, Tiretta left the table, and we sat down all four of us by the fire, where my fresh conquest had an opportunity of shewing her wit. M. le Noir was a man of much intelligence and great experience. He made her talk of the convent where she had been, and as soon as he knew her name he began to speak of her father, with whom he had been well acquainted. He was a councillor of the Parliament of Rouen, and had enjoyed a great reputation during his lifetime.

My sweetheart was above the ordinary height, her hair was a fine golden colour, and her regular features, despite the brilliance of her eyes, expressed candour and modesty. Her dress allowed me to follow all the lines of her figure, and the eyes dwelt pleasantly on the beauty of her form, and on the two spheres which seemed to lament their too close confinement. Although M. le Noir said nothing of all this, it was easy to see that in his own way he admired her perfections no less than I. He left us at eight o'clock, and half an hour afterwards the fat aunt went away followed by her charming niece and the pale man who had come with them. I lost no time in taking leave with Tiretta, who promised the Pope's niece to join her on the morrow, which he did.

Three or four days later I received at my office a letter from Mdlle. de la Meure—the pretty niece. It ran as follows: "Madame, my aunt, my late mother's sister, is a devotee, fond of gaming, rich, stingy, and unjust. She does not like me, and not having succeeded in persuading me to take the veil, she wants to marry me to a wealthy Dunkirk merchant, whom I do not know, but (mark this) whom she does not know any more than I do. The matrimonial agent has praised him very much, and very naturally, as a man must praise his own goods. This gentleman is satisfied with an income of twelve hundred francs per annum, but he promises to leave me in his will no less than a hundred and fifty thousand francs. You must know that by my mother's will my aunt is obliged to pay me on my wedding day twenty-five thousand crowns.

"If what has taken place between us has not made me contemptible in your sight, I offer you my hand and heart with sixty-five thousand francs, and as much more on my aunt's death.

"Don't send me any answer, as I don't know how or by whom to receive your letter. You can answer me in your own person next Sunday at Madame Lambertini's. You will thus have four days whereon to consider this most important question. I do not exactly know whether I love you, but I am quite sure that I prefer you to any other man. I know that each of us has still to gain the other's esteem, but I am sure you would make my life a happy one, and that I should be a faithful wife. If you think that the happiness I seek can add to your own, I must warn you that you will need the aid of a lawyer, as my aunt is miserly, and will stick at trifles.

"If you decide in the affirmative you must find a convent for me to take refuge in before I commit myself to anything, as otherwise I should be exposed to the harsh treatment I wish to avoid. If, on the other hand, my proposal does not meet your views, I have one favour to ask by granting which you will earn my everlasting gratitude. This is that you will endeavour to see me no more, and will take care not to be present in any company in which you think I am to be found. Thus you will help me to forget you, and this is the least you can do for me. You may guess that I shall never be happy till I have become your wife or have forgotten you. Farewell! I reckon upon seeing you on Sunday."

This letter affected me. I felt that it was dictated by prudent, virtuous, and honourable feelings, and I found even more merit in the intellectual endowments of the girl than in her beauty. I blushed at having in a manner led her astray, and I should have thought myself worthy of punishment if I had been capable of refusing the hand offered to me with so much nobility of feeling. And a second but still a powerful consideration made me look complacently upon a fortune larger than I could reasonably expect to win. Nevertheless, the idea of the marriage state, for which I felt I had no vocation, made me tremble.

I knew myself too well not to be aware that as a married man I should be unhappy, and, consequently, with the best intentions I should fail in making the woman's life a happy one. My uncertainty in the four days which she had wisely left me convinced me that I was not in love with her. In spite of that, so weak was I that I could not summon up courage to reject her offer—still less to tell her so frankly, which would have made her esteem me.

During these four days I was entirely absorbed in this one subject. I bitterly repented of having outraged her modesty, for I now esteemed and respected her, but yet I could not make up my mind to repair the wrong I had done her. I could not bear to incur her dislike, but the idea of tying myself down was dreadful to me; and such is the condition of a man who has to choose between two alternatives, and cannot make up his mind.

Fearing lest my evil genius should take me to the opera or elsewhere, and in spite of myself make me miss my appointment, I resolved to dine with the Lambertini without having come to any decision. The pious niece of the Pope was at mass when I reached her house. I found Tiretta engaged in playing on the flute, but as soon as he saw me he dropped the instrument, ran up to me, embraced me, and gave me back the money his suit had cost me.

"I see you are in cash, old fellow; I congratulate you."

"It's a grievous piece of luck to me, for the money is stolen, and I am sorry I have got it though I was an accomplice in the theft."

"What! the money is stolen?"

"Yes, sharping is done here, and I have been taught to help. I share in their ill-gotten gains because I have not the strength of mind to refuse. My landlady and two or three women of the same sort pluck the pigeons. The business does not suit me, and I am thinking of leaving it. Sooner or later I shall kill or be killed, and either event will be the death of me, so I am thinking of leaving this cutthroat place as soon as possible."

"I advise you—nay, I bid you do so by all means, and I should think you had better be gone to-day than to-morrow."

"I don't want to do anything suddenly, as M. le Noir is a gentleman and my friend, and he thinks me a cousin to this wretched woman. As he knows nothing of the infamous trade she carries on, he would suspect something, and perhaps would leave her after learning the reason of my departure. I shall find some excuse or other in the course of the next five or six days, and then I will make haste and return to you."

The Lambertini thanked me for coming to dinner in a friendly manner, and told me that we should have the company of Mdlle. de la Meure and her aunt. I asked her if she was still satisfied with my friend "Sixtimes," and she told me that though the count did not always reside on his manor, she was for all that delighted with him; and said she,

"I am too good a monarch to ask too much of my vassals."

I congratulated her, and we continued to jest till the arrival of the two other guests.

As soon as Mdlle. de la Meure saw me she could scarcely conceal her pleasure. She was in half mourning, and looked so pretty in this costume, which threw up the whiteness of her skin, that I still wonder why that instant did not determine my fate.

Tiretta, who had been making his toilette, rejoined us, and as nothing prevented me from shewing the liking I had taken for the amiable girl I paid her all possible attention. I told the aunt that I found her niece so pretty that I would renounce my bachelorhood if I could find such a mate.

"My niece is a virtuous and sweet-tempered 'girl, sir, but she is utterly devoid either of intelligence or piety."

"Never mind the intelligence," said the niece, "but I was never found wanting in piety at the convent."

"I dare say the nuns are of the jesuitical party."

"What has that got to do with it, aunt?"

"Very much, child; the Jesuits and their adherents are well known to have no vital religion. But let us talk of something else. All that I want you to do is to know how to please your future husband."

"Is mademoiselle about to marry, then?"

"Her intended will probably arrive at the beginning of next month."

"Is he a lawyer?"

"No, sir; he is a well-to-do merchant."

"M. le Noir told me that your niece was the daughter of a councillor, and
I did not imagine that you would sanction her marrying beneath her."

"There will be no question of such a thing in this instance, sir; and, after all, what is marrying beneath one? My niece's intended is an honest, and therefore a noble, man, and I am sure it will be her fault if she does not lead a life of perfect happiness with him."

"Quite so, supposing she loves him."

"Oh! love and all that kind of thing will come in good time, you know."

As these remarks could only give pain to the young lady, who listened in silence, I changed the conversation to the enormous crowd which would be present at the execution of Damien, and finding them extremely desirous of witnessing this horrible sight I offered them a large window with an excellent view. The ladies accepted with great pleasure, and I promised to escort them in good time.

I had no such thing as a window, but I knew that in Paris, as everywhere, money will procure anything. After dinner I went out on the plea of business, and, taking the first coach I came across, in a quarter of an hour I succeeded in renting a first floor window in excellent position for three louis. I paid in advance, taking care to have a receipt.

My business over, I hastened to rejoin the company, and found them engaged in piquet. Mdlle. de la Meure, who knew nothing about it, was tired of looking on. I came up to her, and having something to say we went to the other end of the room.

"Your letter, dearest, has made me the happiest of men. You have displayed in it such intelligence and such admirable characteristics as would win you the fervent adoration of every man of good sense."

"I only want one man's love. I will be content with the esteem of the rest."

"My angel, I will make you my wife, and I shall bless till my latest breath the lucky audacity to which I owe my being chosen before other men who would not have refused your hand, even without the fifty thousand crowns, which are nothing in comparison with your beauty and your wit."

"I am very glad you like me so much."

"Could I do otherwise? And now that you know my heart, do nothing hastily, but trust in me."

"You will not forget how I am placed."

"I will bear it in mind. Let me have time to take a house, to furnish it and to put myself in a position in which I shall be worthy of your hand. You must remember that I am only in furnished apartments; that you are well connected, and that I should not like to be regarded as a fortune-hunter."

"You know that my intended husband will soon arrive?"

"Yes, I will take care of that."

"When he does come, you know, matters will be pushed on rapidly."

"Not too rapidly for me to be able to set you free in twenty-four hours, and without letting your aunt know that the blow comes from me. You may rest assured, dearest, that the minister for foreign affairs, on being assured that you wish to marry me, and me only, will get you an inviolable asylum in the best convent in Paris. He will also retain counsel on your behalf, and if your mother's will is properly drawn out your aunt will soon be obliged to hand over your dowry, and to give security for the rest of the property. Do not trouble yourself about the matter, but let the Dunkirk merchant come when he likes. At all hazards, you may reckon upon me, and you may be sure you will not be in your aunt's house on the day fixed for the wedding."

"I confide in you entirely, but for goodness' sake say no more on a circumstance which wounds my sense of modesty. You said that I offered you marriage because you took liberties with me?"

"Was I wrong?"

"Yes, partly, at all events; and you ought to know that if I had not good reasons I should have done a very foolish thing in offering to marry you, but I may as well tell you that, liberties or no liberties, I should always have liked you better than anyone."

I was beside myself with joy, and seizing her hand I covered it with tender and respectful kisses; and I feel certain that if a notary and priest had been then and there available, I should have married her without the smallest hesitation.

Full of each other, like all lovers, we paid no attention to the horrible racket that was going on at the other end of the room. At last I thought it my duty to see what was happening, and leaving my intended I rejoined the company to quiet Tiretta.

I saw on the table a casket, its lid open, and full of all sorts of jewels; close by were two men who were disputing with Tiretta, who held a book in one hand. I saw at once that they were talking about a lottery, but why were they disputing? Tiretta told me they were a pair of knaves who had won thirty or forty louis of him by means of the book, which he handed to me.

"Sir," said one of the gamesters, "this book treats of a lottery in which all the calculations are made in the fairest manner possible. It contains twelve hundred leaves, two hundred being winning leaves, while the rest are blanks. Anyone who wants to play has only to pay a crown, and then to put a pin's point at random between two leaves of the closed book. The book is then opened at the place where the pin is, and if the leaf is blank the player loses; but if, on the other hand, the leaf bears a number, he is given the corresponding ticket, and an article of the value indicated on the ticket is then handed to him. Please to observe, sir, that the lowest prize is twelve francs, and there are some numbers worth as much as six hundred francs, and even one to the value of twelve hundred. We have been playing for an hour, and have lost several costly articles, and madam," pointing to my sweetheart's aunt, "has won a ring worth six louis, but as she preferred cash, she continued playing and lost the money she had gained."

"Yes," said the aunt, "and these gentlemen have won everybody's money with their accursed game; which proves it is all a mere cheat."

"It proves they are rogues," said Tiretta.

"But gentlemen," answered one of them, "in that case the receivers of the Government lottery are rogues too"; whereon Tiretta gave him a box on the ear. I threw myself between the two combatants, and told them not to speak a word.

"All lotteries," said I, "are advantageous to the holders, but the king is at the head of the Government lottery, and I am the principal receiver, in which character I shall proceed to confiscate this casket, and give you the choice of the following alternatives: You can, if you like, return to the persons present the money you have unlawfully won from them, whereupon I will let you go with your box. If you refuse to do so, I shall send for a policeman, who will take you to prison, and to-morrow you will be tried by M. Berier, to whom I shall take this book in the morning. We shall soon see whether we are rogues as well as they."

Seeing that they had to do with a man of determination, and that resistance would only result in their losing all, they resolved with as good a grace as they could muster to return all their winnings, and for all I know double the sum, for they were forced to return forty louis, though they swore they had only won twenty. The company was too select for me to venture to decide between them. In point of fact I was rather inclined to believe the rascals, but I was angry with them, and I wanted them to pay a good price for having made a comparison, quite right in the main, but odious to me in the extreme. The same reason, doubtless, prevented me from giving them back their book, which I had no earthly right to keep, and which they asked me in vain to return to them. My firmness and my threats, and perhaps also the fear of the police, made them think themselves lucky to get off with their jewel-box. As soon as they were gone the ladies, like the kindly creatures they were, began to pity them. "You might have given them back their book," they said to me.

"And you, ladies, might have let them keep their money."

"But they cheated us of it."

"Did they? Well, their cheating was done with the book, and I have done them a kindness by taking it from them."

They felt the force of my remarks, and the conversation took another turn.

Early next morning the two gamesters paid me a visit bringing with them as a bribe a beautiful casket containing twenty-four lovely pieces of Dresden china. I found this argument irresistible, and I felt obliged to return them the book, threatening them at the same time with imprisonment if they dared to carry on their business in Paris for the future. They promised me to abstain from doing so—no doubt with a mental reservation, but I cared nothing about that.

I resolved to offer this beautiful gift to Mdlle. de la Meure, and I took it to her the same day. I had a hearty welcome, and the aunt loaded me with thanks.

On March the 28th, the day of Damien's martyrdom, I went to fetch the ladies in good time; and as the carriage would scarcely hold us all, no objection was made to my taking my sweetheart on my knee, and in this order we reached the Place de Greve. The three ladies packing themselves together as tightly as possible took up their positions at the window, leaning forward on their elbows, so as to prevent us seeing from behind. The window had two steps to it, and they stood on the second; and in order to see we had to stand on the same step, for if we had stood on the first we should not have been able to see over their heads. I have my reasons for giving these minutiae, as otherwise the reader would have some difficulty in guessing at the details which I am obliged to pass over in silence.

We had the courage to watch the dreadful sight for four hours. The circumstances of Damien's execution are too well known to render it necessary for me to speak of them; indeed, the account would be too long a one, and in my opinion such horrors are an offence to our common humanity.

Damien was a fanatic, who, with the idea of doing a good work and obtaining a heavenly reward, had tried to assassinate Louis XV.; and though the attempt was a failure, and he only gave the king a slight wound, he was torn to pieces as if his crime had been consummated.

While this victim of the Jesuits was being executed, I was several times obliged to turn away my face and to stop my ears as I heard his piercing shrieks, half of his body having been torn from him, but the Lambertini and the fat aunt did not budge an inch. Was it because their hearts were hardened? They told me, and I pretended to believe them, that their horror at the wretch's wickedness prevented Them feeling that compassion which his unheard-of torments should have excited. The fact was that Tiretta kept the pious aunt curiously engaged during the whole time of the execution, and this, perhaps, was what prevented the virtuous lady from moving or even turning her head round.

Finding himself behind her, he had taken the precaution to lift up her dress to avoid treading on it. That, no doubt, was according to the rule; but soon after, on giving an involuntary glance in their direction, I found that Tiretta had carried his precautions rather far, and, not wishing to interrupt my friend or to make the lady feel awkward, I turned my head and stood in such a way that my sweetheart could see nothing of what was going on; this put the good lady at her ease. For two hours after I heard a continuous rustling, and relishing the joke I kept quiet the whole time. I admired Tiretta's hearty appetite still more than his courage, but what pleased me most was the touching resignation with which the pious aunt bore it all.

At the end of this long session I saw Madame turn round, and doing the same I fixed my gaze on Tiretta, and found him looking as fresh and cool as if nothing had happened, but the aunt seemed to me to have a rather pensive appearance. She had been under the fatal necessity of keeping quiet and letting Tiretta do what he liked for fear of the Lambertini's jests, and lest her niece might be scandalized by the revelation of mysteries of which she was supposed to know nothing.

We set out, and having dropped the Pope's niece at her door, I begged her to lend me Tiretta for a few hours, and I then took Madame to her house in the Rue St. Andre-des-Arts. She asked me to come and see her the following day as she had something to tell me, and I remarked that she took no notice of my friend as she left us. We went to the "Hotel de Russie," where they gave you an excellent dinner for six francs a head, and I thought my mad friend stood in need of recruiting his strength.

"What were you doing behind Madame—?" said I.

"I am sure you saw nothing, or anybody else either."

"No, because when I saw the beginning of your manoeuvres, and guessed what was coming, I stood in such a way that neither the Lambertini or the pretty niece could see you. I can guess what your goal was, and I must say I admire your hearty appetite. But your wretched victim appears to be rather angry."

"Oh! my dear fellow, that's all the affectation of an old maid. She may pretend to be put out, but as she kept quiet the whole time I am certain she would be glad to begin all over again."

"I think so, too, in her heart of hearts; but her pride might suggest that you had been lacking in respect, and the suggestion would be by no means groundless."

"Respect, you say; but must one not always be lacking in respect to women when one wants to come to the point?"

"Quite so, but there's a distinction between what lovers may do when they are together, and what is proper in the presence of a mixed company."

"Yes, but I snatched four distinct favours from her, without the least opposition; had I not therefore good reasons for taking her consent for granted?"

"You reason well, but you see she is out of humour with you. She wants to speak to me to-morrow, and I have no doubt that you will be the subject of our conversation."

"Possibly, but still I should think she would not speak to you of the comic piece of business; it would be very silly of her."

"Why so? You don't know these pious women. They are brought up by Jesuits, who often give them some good lessons on the subject, and they are delighted to confess to a third party; and these confessions with a seasoning of tears gives them in their own eyes quite a halo of saintliness."

"Well, let her tell you if she likes. We shall see what comes of it."

"Possibly she may demand satisfaction; in which case I shall be glad to do my best for her."

"You make me laugh! I can't imagine what sort of satisfaction she could claim, unless she wants to punish me by the 'Lex talionis', which would be hardly practicable without a repetition of the original offence. If she had not liked the game, all she had to do was to give me a push which would have sent me backwards."

"Yes, but that would have let us know what you had been trying to do."

"Well, if it comes to that, the slightest movement would have rendered the whole process null and void; but as it was she stood in the proper position as quiet as a lamb; nothing could be easier."

"It's an amusing business altogether. But did you notice that the Lambertini was angry with you, too? She, perhaps, saw what you were doing, and felt hurt."

"Oh! she has got another cause of complaint against me. We have fallen out, and I am leaving her this evening."

"Really?"

"Yes, I will tell you all about it. Yesterday evening, a young fellow in the Inland Revenue who had been seduced to sup with us by a hussy of Genoa, after losing forty louis, threw, the cards in the face of my landlady and called her a thief. On the impulse of the moment I took a candle and put it out on his face. I might have destroyed one of his eyes, but I fortunately hit him on the cheek. He immediately ran for his sword, mine was ready, and if the Genoese had not thrown herself between us murder might have been committed. When the poor wretch saw his cheek in the glass, he became so furious that nothing short of the return of all his money would appease him. They gave it him back, in spite of my advice, for in doing so they admitted, tacitly at all events, that it had been won by cheating. This caused a sharp dispute between the Lambertini and myself after he had gone. She said we should have kept the forty louis, and nothing would have happened except for my interference, that it was her and not me whom the young man had insulted. The Genoese added that if we had kept cool we should have had the plucking of him, but that God alone knew what he would do now with the mark of the burn on his face. Tired of the talk of these infamous women, I was about to leave them, but my landlady began to ride the high horse, and went so far as to call me a beggar.

"If M. le Noir had not come in just then, she would have had a bad time of it, as my stick was already in my hand. As soon as they saw him they told me to hold my tongue, but my blood was up; and turning towards the worthy man I told him that his mistress had called me a beggar, that she was a common prostitute, that I was not her cousin, nor in any way related to her, and that I should leave her that very day. As soon as I had come to the end of this short and swift discourse, I went out and shut myself up in my room. In the course of the next two hours I shall go and fetch my linen, and I hope to breakfast with you to-morrow."

Tiretta did well. His heart was in the right place, and he was wise not to allow the foolish impulses of youth to plunge him in the sink of corruption. As long as a man has not committed a dishonourable action, as long as his heart is sound, though his head may go astray, the path of duty is still open to him. I should say the same of women if prejudice were not so strong in their case, and if they were not much more under the influence of the heart than the head.

After a good dinner washed down by some delicious Sillery we parted, and I spent the evening in writing. Next morning I did some business, and at noon went to see the distressed devotee, whom I found at home with her charming niece. We talked a few minutes about the weather, and she then told my sweetheart to leave us as she wanted to speak to me. I was prepared for what was coming and I waited for her to break the silence which all women of her position observe. "You will be surprised, sir, at what I am going to tell you, for I have determined to bring before you a complaint of an unheard-of character. The case is really of the most delicate nature, and I am impelled to make a confidant of you by the impression you made on me when I first saw you. I consider you to be a man of discretion, of honour, and above all a moral man; in short, I believe you have experienced religion, and if I am making a mistake it will be a pity, for though I have been insulted I don't lack means of avenging myself, and as you are his friend you will be sorry for him."

"Is Tiretta the guilty party, madam?"

"The same."

"And what is his crime?"

"He is a villain; he has insulted me in the most monstrous manner."

"I should not have thought him capable of doing so."

"I daresay not, but then you are a moral man."

"But what was the nature of his offence? You may confide in my secrecy."

"I really couldn't tell you, it's quite out of the question; but I trust you will be able to guess it. Yesterday, during the execution of the wretched Damien, he strongly abused the position in which he found himself behind me."

"I see; I understand what you mean; you need say no more. You have cause for anger, and he is to blame for acting in such a manner. But allow me to say that the case is not unexampled or even uncommon, and I think you might make some allowance for the strength of love, the close quarters, and above all for the youth and passion of the sinner. Moreover, the offence is one which may be expiated in a number of ways, provided the parties come to an agreement. Tiretta is young and a perfect gentleman, he is handsome and at bottom a good fellow; could not a marriage be arranged?"

I waited for a reply, but perceiving that the injured party kept silence (a circumstance which seemed to me a good omen) I went on.

"If marriage should not meet your views, we might try a lasting friendship, in which he could shew his repentance and prove himself deserving of pardon. Remember, madam, that Tiretta is only a man, and therefore subject to all the weaknesses of our poor human nature; and even you have your share of the blame."

"I, sir?"

"Involuntarily, madam, involuntarily; not you but your charms led him astray. Nevertheless, without this incentive the circumstance would never have taken place, and I think you should consider your beauty as a mitigation of the offence."

"You plead your cause well, sir, but I will do you justice and confess that all your remarks have been characterized by much

Christian feeling. However, you are reasoning on false premises; you are ignorant of his real crime, yet how should you guess it?"

With this she burst into tears, leading me completely off the scent, and not knowing what to think.

"He can't have stolen her purse," said I to myself, "as I don't think him capable of such an action; and if I did I'd blow his brains out."

The afflicted lady soon dried her tears, and went on as follows:

"You are thinking of a deed which one might possibly succeed in reconciling with reason, and in making amends for; but the crime of which that brute has been guilty I dare scarcely imagine, as it is almost enough to drive me mad."

"Good heavens! you can't mean it? This is dreadful; do I hear you aright?"

"Yes. You are moved, I see, but such are the circumstances of the case. Pardon my tears, which flow from anger and the shame with which I am covered."

"Yes, and from outraged religion, too."

"Certainly, certainly. That is the chief source of my grief, and I should have mentioned it if I had not feared you were not so strongly attached to religion as myself."

"Nobody, God be praised! could be more strongly attached to religion than
I, and nothing can ever unloose the ties which bind me to it:"

"You will be grieved, then, to hear that I am destined to suffer eternal punishment, for I must and will be avenged."

"Not so, madam, perish the thought, as I could not become your accomplice in such a design, and if you will not abandon it at least say nothing to me on the subject. I will promise you to tell him nothing, although as he lives with me the sacred laws of hospitality oblige me to give him due warning."

"I thought he lived with the Lambertini"

"He left her yesterday. The connection between them was a criminal one, and I have drawn him back from the brink of the precipice."

"You don't mean to say so!"

"Yes, upon my word of honour."

"You astonish one. This is very edifying. I don't wish the young man's death, but you must confess he owes me some reparation."

"He does indeed. A charming Frenchwoman is not to be handled in the Italian manner without signal amends, but I can think of nothing at all commensurate with the offence. There is only one plan, which I will endeavour to carry out if you will agree to it."

"What is that?"

"I will put the guilty party in your power without his knowing what is to happen, and I will leave you alone, so that you can wreak all your wrath upon him, provided you will allow me to be, unknown to him, in the next room, as I shall regard myself as responsible for his safety."

"I consent. You will stay in this room, and he must be left in the other where I shall receive you, but take care he has no suspicion of your presence."

"He shan't dream of it. He will not even know where I am taking him, for he must not think that I have been informed of his misdoings. As soon as we be there, and the conversation becomes general, I shall leave the room, pretending to be going away."

"When will you bring him? I long to cover him with confusion. I will make him tremble. I am curious to hear how he will justify himself for such an offence."

"I can't say, but I think and hope that your presence will make him eloquent, as I should like to see your differences adjusted."

At one o'clock the Abbe des Forges arrived, and she made me sit down to dinner with them. This abbe was a pupil of the famous Bishop of Auxerre, who was still living. I talked so well on the subject of grace, and made so many quotations from St. Augustine, that the abbe and the devotee took me for a zealous Jansenista character with which my dress and appearance did not at all correspond. My sweetheart did not give me a single glance while the meal was going on, and thinking she had some motives I abstained from speaking to her.

After dinner, which, by the way, was a very good one, I promised the offended lady to bring her the culprit bound hand and foot next day, after the play was over. To put her at her ease I said I should walk, as I was certain that he would not recognize the house in the dark.

As soon as I saw Tiretta, I began with a seriocomic air to reproach him for the dreadful crime he had committed on the body of a lady in every way virtuous and respectable, but the mad fellow began to laugh, and it would have been waste of time for me to try to stop him.

"What!" said he, "she has had the courage to tell you all?"

"You don't deny the fact, then?"

"If she says it is so, I don't think I can give her the lie, but I am ready to swear that I don't know how the land lay. In the position I was in it was impossible for me to say where I took up my dwelling. However, I will quiet her indignation, as I shall come to the point quickly, and not let her wait."

"You will ruin the business if you don't take care; be as long as you can; she will like that best, and it will be to your interest. Don't hurry yourself, and never mind me, as I am sure to get on all right while you are changing anger into a softer passion. Remember not to know that I am in the house, and if you only stay with her a short time (which I don't think will be the case) take a coach and be off. You know the least a pious woman like her can do will be to provide me with fire and company. Don't forget that she is well-born like yourself. These women of quality are, no doubt, as immoral as any other women, since they are constructed of the same material, but they like to have their pride flattered by certain attentions. She is rich, a devote, and, what is more, inclined to pleasure; strive to gain her friendship 'faciem ad faciem', as the King of Prussia says. You may, perhaps, make your fortune."

"If she asks you why you have left the Pope's niece, take care not to tell her the reason. She will be pleased with your discretion. In short, do your best to expiate the enormity of your offence."

"I have only to speak the truth. I went in in the dark."

"That's an odd reason, but it may seem convincing to a Frenchwoman."

I need not tell the reader that I gave Tiretta a full account of my conversation with the lady. If any complain of this breach of honour, I must tell them that I had made a mental reservation not to keep my promise, and those who are acquainted with the morality of the children of Ignatius will understand that I was completely at my ease.

Next day we went to the opera, and afterwards, our plans made out, we walked to the house of the insulted and virtuous lady. She received us with great dignity, but yet there was an agreeable undercurrent in her voice and manner which I thought very promising.

"I never take supper," she said, "but if you had forewarned me of your visit I should have got something for you."

After telling her all the news I had heard in the theatre, I pretended to be obliged to go, and begged her to let me leave the count with her for a few minutes.

"If I am more than a quarter of an hour," said I to the count, "don't wait. Take a coach home and we shall see each other to-morrow."

Instead of going downstairs I went into the next room, and two minutes after who should enter but my sweetheart, who looked charmed and yet puzzled at my appearance.

"I think I must be dreaming," said she, "but my aunt has charged me not to leave you alone, and to tell her woman not to come upstairs unless she rings the bell. Your friend is with her, and she told me to speak low as he is not to know that you are here. What does it all mean?"

"You are curious, are you?"

"I confess I am in this instance, for all this mystery seems designed to excite curiosity."

"Dearest, you shall know all; but how cold it is."

"My aunt has told me to make a good fire, she has become liberal or rather lavish all of a sudden; look at the wax candles."

"That's a new thing, is it?"

"Oh, quite new."

As soon as we were seated in front of the fire I began to tell her the story, to which she listened with all the attention a young girl can give to such a matter; but as I had thought it well to pass over some of the details, she could not properly understand what crime it was that Tiretta had committed. I was not sorry to be obliged to tell her the story in plain language, and to give more expression I employed the language of gesture, which made her blush and laugh at the same time. I then told her that, having taken up the question of the reparation that was due to her aunt, I had so arranged matters that I was certain of being alone with her all the time my friend was engaged. Thereupon I began to cover her pretty face with kisses, and as I allowed myself no other liberties she received my caresses as a proof of the greatness of my love and the purity of my feelings.

"Dearest," she said, "what you say puzzles me; there are two things which I can't understand. How could Tiretta succeed in committing this crime with my aunt, which I think would only be possible with the consent of the party attacked, but quite impossible without it; and this makes me believe that if the thing was done it was done with her hearty good will."

"Very true, for if she did not like it she had only to change her position."

"Not so much as that; she need only have kept the door shut."

"There, sweetheart, you are wrong, for a properly-made man only asks you to keep still and he will overcome all obstacles. Moreover, I don't expect that your aunt's door is so well shut as yours."

"I believe that I could defy all the Tirettas in the world.

"There's another thing I don't understand, and that is how my blessed aunt came to tell you all about it; for if she had any sense she might have known that it would only make you laugh. And what satisfaction does she expect to get from a brute like that, who possibly thinks the affair a matter of no consequence. I should think he would do the same to any woman who occupied the same position as my aunt."

"You are right, for he told me he went in like a blind man, not knowing where he was going."

"Your friend is a queer fellow, and if other men are like him I am sure I should have no feeling but contempt for them."

"She has told me nothing about the satisfaction she is thinking of, and which she possibly feels quite sure of attaining; but I think I can guess what it will be namely, a formal declaration of love; and I suppose he will expiate his crime by becoming her lover, and doubtless this will be their wedding night."

"The affair is getting amusing. I can't believe it. My dear aunt is too anxious about her salvation; and how do you imagine the young man can ever fall in love with her, or play the part with such a face as hers before his eyes. Have you ever seen a countenance as disgusting as my aunt's? Her skin is covered with pimples, her eyes distil humours, and her teeth and breath are enough to discourage any man. She's hideous."

"All that is nothing to a young spark of twenty-five; one is always ready for an assault at that age; not like me who only feel myself a man in presence of charms like yours, of which I long to be the lawful possessor."

"You will find me the most affectionate of wives, and I feel quite sure that I shall have your heart in such good keeping that I shall never be afraid of losing it."

We had talked thus pleasantly for an hour, and Tiretta was still with the aunt. I thought things pointed towards a reconciliation, and judged the matter was getting serious. I told my sweetheart my opinion, and asked her to give me something to eat.

"I can only give you," said she, "some bread and cheese, a slice of ham, and some wine which my aunt pronounces excellent."

"Bring them quick, then; I am fainting with hunger."

She soon laid the table for two, and put on it all the food she had. The cheese was Roquefort, and the ham had been covered with jelly. About ten persons with reasonable appetites should have been able to sup on what there was; but (how I know not) the whole disappeared, and also two bottles of Chambertin, which I seem to taste now. My sweetheart's eyes gleamed with pleasure: truly Chambertin and Roquefort are excellent thinks to restore an old love and to ripen a young one.

"Don't you want to know what your aunt has been doing the last two hours with M. Sixtimes?"

"They are playing, perhaps; but there is a small hole in the wall, and I will look and see. I can only see the two candles, and the wicks are an inch long."

"Didn't I say so? Give me a coverlet and I will sleep on the sofa here, and do you go to bed. But let me look at it first."

She made me come into her little room, where I saw a pretty bed, a prayer desk, and a large crucifix.

"Your bed is too small for you, dear heart."

"Oh, not at all! I am very comfortable"; and so saying she laid down at full length.

"What a beautiful wife I shall have! Nay, don't move, let me look at you so." My hand began to press the bosom of her dress, where were imprisoned two spheres which seemed to lament their captivity. I went farther, I began to untie strings . . . for where does desire stop short?

"Sweetheart, I cannot resist, but you will not love me afterwards."

"I will always love you."

Soon her beautiful breasts were exposed to my burning kisses. The flame of my love lit another in her heart, and forgetting her former self she opened her arms to me, making me promise not to despise her, and what would one not promise! The modesty inherent in the sex, the fear of results, perhaps a kind of instinct which reveals to them the natural faithlessness of men make women ask for such promises, but what mistress, if really amorous, would even think of asking her lover to respect her in the moment of delirious ecstacy, when all one's being is centred on the fulfilment of desire?

After we had passed an hour in these amorous toyings, which set my sweetheart on fire, her charms having never before been exposed to the burning lips or the free caresses of a man, I said to her,

"I grieve to leave you without having rendered to your beauty the greatest homage which it deserves so well."

A sigh was her only answer.

It was cold, the fire was out, and I had to spend the night on the sofa.

"Give me a coverlet, dearest, that I may go away from you, for I should die here between love and cold if you made me abstain."

"Lie where I have been, sweetheart. I will get up and rekindle the fire."

She got up in all her naked charms, and as she put a stick to the fire the flame leapt up; I rose, I found her standing so as to display all her beauties, and I could refrain no longer. I pressed her to my heart, she returned my caresses, and till day-break we gave ourselves up to an ecstacy of pleasure.

We had spent four or five delicious hours on the sofa. She then left me, and after making a good fire she went to her room, and I remained on the sofa and slept till noon. I was awakened by Madame, who wore a graceful undress.

"Still asleep, M. Casanova?"

"Ah! good morning, madam, good morning. And what has become of my friend?"

"He has become mine, I have forgiven him."

"What has he done to be worthy of so generous a pardon?"

"He proved to me that he made a mistake."

"I am delighted to hear it; where is he?"

"He has gone home, where you will find him; but don't say anything about your spending the night here, or he will think it was spent with my niece. I am very much obliged to you for what you have done, and I have only to ask you to be discreet."

"You can count on me entirely, for I am grateful to you for having forgiven my friend."

"Who would not do so? The dear young man is something more than mortal. If you knew how he loved me! I am grateful to him, and I have taken him to board for a year; he will be well lodged, well fed, and so on."

"What a delightful plan! You have arranged the terms, I suppose."

"All that will be settled in a friendly way, and we shall not need to have recourse to arbitration. We shall set out to-day for Villette, where I have a nice little house; for you know that it is necessary, at first, to act in such a way as to give no opportunity to slanderers. My lover will have all he wants, and whenever you, sir, honour us with your presence you will find a pretty room and a good bed at your disposal. All I am sorry for is that you will find it tedious; my poor niece is so dull."

"Madam, your niece is delightful; she gave me yesterday evening an excellent supper and kept me company till three o'clock this morning."

"Really? I can't make it out how she gave you anything, as there was nothing in the house."

"At any rate, madam, she gave me an excellent supper, of which there are no remains, and after keeping me company she went to bed, and I have had a good night on this comfortable sofa."

"I am glad that you, like myself, were pleased with everything, but I did not think my niece so clever."

"She is very clever, madam—in my eyes, at all events."

"Oh, sir! you are a judge of wit, let us go and see her. She has locked her door. Come open the door, why have you shut yourself up, you little prude? what are you afraid of. My Casanova is incapable of hurting you."

The niece opened her door and apologized for the disorder of her dress, but what costume could have suited her better? Her costume was dazzling."

"There she is," said the aunt, "and she is not so bad looking after all, but it is a pity she is so stupid. You were very right to give this gentleman a supper. I am much obliged to you for doing so. I have been playing all night, and when one is playing one only thinks of the game. I have determined on taking young Tiretta to board with us. He is an excellent and clever young man, and I am sure he will learn to speak French before long. Get dressed, my dear, as we must begin to pack. We shall set out this afternoon for Villette, and shall spend there the whole of the spring. There is no need, you know, to say anything about this to my sister:"

"I, aunt? Certainly not. Did I ever tell her anything on the other occasions?"

"Other occasions! You see what a silly girl it is. Do you mean by 'other occasions,' that I have been circumstanced like this before?"

"No, aunt. I only meant to say that I had never told her anything of what you did."

"That's right, my dear, but you must learn to express yourself properly. We dine at two, and I hope to have the pleasure of M. Casanova's company at dinner; we will start immediately after the meal. Tiretta promised to bring his small portmanteau with him, and it will go with our luggage."

After promising to dine with them, I bade the ladies good-bye; and I went home as fast as I could walk, for I was as curious as a woman to know what arrangements had been made.

"Well," said I to Tiretta, "I find you have got a place. Tell me all about it."

"My dear fellow, I have sold myself for a year. My pay is to be twenty-five louis a month, a good table, good lodging, etc., etc."

"I congratulate you."

"Do you think it is worth the trouble?"

"There's no rose without a thorn. She told me you were something more than mortal."

"I worked hard all night to prove it to her; but I am quite sure your time was better employed than mine."

"I slept like a king. Dress yourself, as I am coming to dinner, and I want to see you set out for Villette. I shall come and see you there now and then, as your sweetheart has told me that a room shall be set apart for my convenience."

We arrived at two o'clock. Madame dressed in a girlish style presented a singular appearance, but Mdlle. de la Meure's beauty shone like a star. Love and pleasure had given her a new life, a new being. We had a capital dinner, as the good lady had made the repast dainty like herself; but in the dishes there was nothing absurd, while her whole appearance was comic in the highest degree. At four they all set out, and I spent my evening at the Italian comedy.

I was in love with Mdlle. de la Meure, but Silvia's daughter, whose company at supper was all I had of her, weakened a love which now left nothing more to desire.

We complain of women who, though loving us and sure of our love, refuse us their favours; but we are wrong in doing so, for if they love they have good reason to fear lest they lose us in the moment of satisfying our desires. Naturally they should do all in their power to retain our hearts, and the best way to do so is to cherish our desire of possessing them; but desire is only kept alive by being denied: enjoyment kills it, since one cannot desire what one has got. I am, therefore, of opinion that women are quite right to refuse us. But if it be granted that the passions of the two sexes are of equal strength, how comes it that a man never refuses to gratify a woman who loves him and entreats him to be kind?

We cannot receive the argument founded on the fear of results, as that is a particular and not a general consideration. Our conclusion, then, will be that the reason lies in the fact that a man thinks more of the pleasure he imparts than that which he receives, and is therefore eager to impart his bliss to another. We know, also, that, as a general rule, women, when once enjoyed, double their love and affection. On the other hand, women think more of the pleasure they receive than of that which they impart, and therefore put off enjoyment as long as possible, since they fear that in giving themselves up they lose their chief good—their own pleasure. This feeling is peculiar to the sex, and is the only cause of coquetry, pardonable in a woman, detestable in a man.

Silvia's daughter loved me, and she knew I loved her, although I had never said so, but women's wit is keen. At the same time she endeavoured not to let me know her feelings, as she was afraid of encouraging me to ask favours of her, and she did not feel sure of her strength to refuse them; and she knew my inconstant nature. Her relations intended her for Clement, who had been teaching her the clavichord for the last three years. She knew of the arrangement and had no objection, for though she did not love him she liked him very well. Most girls are wedded without love, and they are not sorry for it afterwards. They know that by marriage they become of some consequence in the world, and they marry to have a house of their own and a good position in society. They seem to know that a husband and a lover need not be synonymous terms. At Paris men are actuated by the same views, and most marriages are matters of convenience. The French are jealous of their mistresses, but never of their wives.

There could be no doubt that M. Clement was very much in love, and Mdlle. Baletti was delighted that I noticed it, as she thought this would bring me to a declaration, and she was quite right. The departure of Mdlle. de la Meure had a good deal to do with my determination to declare myself; and I was very sorry to have done so afterwards, for after I had told her I loved her Clement was dismissed, and my position was worse than before. The man who declares his love for a woman in words wants to be sent to school again.

Three days after the departure of Tiretta, I took him what small belongings he had, and Madame seemed very glad to see me. The Abbe des Forges arrived just as we were sitting down to dinner, and though he had been very friendly to me at Paris he did not so much as look at me all through the meal, and treated Tiretta in the same way. I, for my part, took no notice of him, but Tiretta, not so patient as I, at last lost his temper and got up, begging Madame to tell him when she was going to have that fellow to dine with her. We rose from table without saying a word, and the silent abbe went with madam into another room.

Tiretta took me to see his room, which was handsomely furnished, and, as was right, adjoined his sweetheart's. Whilst he was putting his things in order, Mdlle. de la Meure made me come and see my apartment. It was a very nice room on the ground floor, and facing hers. I took care to point out to her how easily I could pay her a visit after everyone was in bed, but she said we should not be comfortable in her room, and that she would consequently save me the trouble of getting out of bed. It will be guessed that I had no objections to make to this arrangement.

She then told me of her aunt's folly about Tiretta.

"She believes," said she, "that we do not know he sleeps with her."

"Believes, or pretends to believe."

"Possibly. She rang for me at eleven o'clock this morning and told me to go and ask him what kind of night he had passed. I did so, but seeing his bed had not been slept in I asked him if he had not been to sleep.

"'No,' said he, 'I have been writing all night, but please don't say anything about it to your aunt: I promised with all my heart to be as silent as the grave.'"

"Does he make sheep's eyes at you?"

"No, but if he did it would be all the same. Though he is not over sharp he knows, I think, what I think of him."

"Why have you such a poor opinion of him?"

"Why? My aunt pays him. I think selling one's self is a dreadful idea."

"But you pay me."

"Yes, but in the same coin as you give me."

The old aunt was always calling her niece stupid, but on the contrary I thought her very clever, and as virtuous as clever. I should never have seduced her if she had not been brought up in a convent.

I went back to Tiretta, and had some pleasant conversation with him. I asked him how he liked his place.

"I don't like it much, but as it costs me nothing I am not absolutely wretched."

"But her face!"

"I don't look at it, and there's one thing I like about her—she is so clean."

"Does she take good care of you?"

"O yes, she is full of feeling for me. This morning she refused the greeting I offered her. 'I am sure,' said she, 'that my refusal will pain you, but your health is so dear to me that I feel bound to look after it.'"

As soon as the gloomy Abbe des Forges was gone and Madame was alone, we rejoined her. She treated me as her gossip, and played the timid child for Tiretta's benefit, and he played up to her admirably, much to my admiration.

"I shall see no more of that foolish priest," said she; "for after telling me that I was lost both in this world and the next he threatened to abandon me, and I took him at his word."

An actress named Quinault, who had left the stage and lived close by, came to call, and soon after Madame Favart and the Abbe de Voisenon arrived, followed by Madame Amelin with a handsome lad named Calabre, whom she called her nephew. He was as like her as two peas, but she did not seem to think that a sufficient reason for confessing she was his mother. M. Patron, a Piedmontese, who also came with her, made a bank at faro and in a couple of hours won everybody's money with the exception of mine, as I knew better than to play. My time was better occupied in the company of my sweet mistress. I saw through the Piedmontese, and had put him down as a knave; but Tiretta was not so sharp, and consequently lost all the money he had in his pockets and a hundred louis besides. The banker having reaped a good harvest put down the cards, and Tiretta told him in good Italian that he was a cheat, to which the Piedmontese replied with the greatest coolness that he lied. Thinking that the quarrel might have an unpleasant ending, I told him that Tiretta was only jesting, and I made my friend say so, too. He then left the company and went to his room.

Eight years afterwards I saw this Patron at St. Petersburg, and in the year 1767 he was assassinated in Poland.

The same evening I preached Tiretta a severe yet friendly sermon. I pointed out to him that when he played he was at the mercy of the banker, who might be a rogue but a man of courage too, and so in calling him a cheat he was risking his life.

"Am I to let myself be robbed, then?"

"Yes, you have a free choice in the matter; nobody will make you play."

"I certainly will not pay him that hundred louis."

"I advise you to do so, and to do so before you are asked."

"You have a knack of persuading one to do what you will, even though one be disposed to take no notice of your advice."

"That's because I speak from heart and head at once, and have some experience in these affairs as well."

Three quarters of an hour afterwards I went to bed and my mistress came to me before long. We spent a sweeter night than before, for it is often a matter of some difficulty to pluck the first flower; and the price which most men put on this little trifle is founded more on egotism than any feeling of pleasure.

Next day, after dining with the family and admiring the roses on my sweetheart's cheeks, I returned to Paris. Three or four days later Tiretta came to tell me that the Dunkirk merchant had arrived, that he was coming to dine at Madame's, and that she requested me to make one of the party. I was prepared for the news, but the blood rushed into my face. Tiretta saw it, and to a certain extent divined my feelings. "You are in love with the niece," said he.

"Why do you think so?"

"By the mystery you make about her; but love betrays itself even by its silence."

"You are a knowing fellow, Tiretta. I will come to dinner, but don't say a word to anybody."

My heart was rent in twain. Possibly if the merchant had put off his arrival for a month I should have welcomed it; but to have only just lifted the nectar to my lips, and to see the precious vessel escape from my hands! To this day I can recall my feelings, and the very recollection is not devoid of bitterness.

I was in a fearful state of perplexity, as I always was whenever it was necessary for me to resolve, and I felt that I could not do so. If the reader has been placed in the same position he will understand my feelings. I could not make up my mind to consent to her marrying, nor could I resolve to wed her myself and gain certain happiness.

I went to Villette and was a little surprised to find Mdlle. de la Meure more elaborately dressed than usual.

"Your intended," I said, "would have pronounced you charming without all that."

"My aunt doesn't think so"

"You have not seen him yet?"

"No, but I should like to, although I trust with your help never to become his wife."

Soon after, she arrived with Corneman, the banker, who had been the agent in this business transaction. The merchant was a fine man, about forty, with a frank and open face. His dress was good though not elaborate. He introduced himself simply but in a polite manner to Madame, and he did not look at his future wife till the aunt presented her to him. His manner immediately became more pleasing; and without making use of flowers of speech he said in a very feeling way that he trusted the impression he had made on her was equal to that which she had made on him. Her only answer was a low curtsy, but she studied him carefully.

Dinner was served, and in the course of the meal we talked of almost everything—except marriage. The happy pair only caught each other's eyes by chance, and did not speak to one another. After dinner Mdlle. de la Meure went to her room, and the aunt went into her closet with the banker and the merchant, and they were in close conversation for two hours. At the end of that time the gentlemen were obliged to return to Paris, and Madame, after summoning her niece, told the merchant she would expect him to dinner on the day following, and that she was sure that her niece would be glad to see him again.

"Won't you, my dear?"

"Yes, aunt, I shall be very glad to see the gentleman again."

If she had not answered thus, the merchant would have gone away without hearing his future bride speak.

"Well," said the aunt, "what do you think of your husband?"

"Allow me to put off my answer till to-morrow; but be good enough, when we are at table, to draw me into the conversation, for it is very possible that my face has not repelled him, but so far he knows nothing of my mental powers; possibly my want of wit may destroy any slight impression my face may have made."

"Yes, I am afraid you will begin to talk nonsense, and make him lose the good opinion he seems to have formed of you."

"It is not right to deceive anybody. If he is disabused of his fictitious ideas by the appearance of the truth, so much the better for him; and so much the worse for both of us, if we decide on marrying without the slightest knowledge of each other's habits and ways of thought."

"What do you think of him?"

"I think he is rather nice-looking, and his manners are kind and polite; but let us wait till to-morrow."

"Perhaps he will have nothing more to say to me; I am so stupid."

"I know very well that you think yourself very clever, and that's where your fault lies; it's your self-conceit which makes you stupid, although M. Casanova takes you for a wit."

"Perhaps he may know what he is talking about."

"My poor dear, he is only laughing at you."

"I have good reasons for thinking otherwise, aunt."

"There you go; you will never get any sense."

"Pardon me, madam, if I cannot be of your opinion. Mademoiselle is quite right in saying that I do not laugh at her. I dare to say that to-morrow she will shine in the conversation."

"You think so? I am glad to hear it. Now let us have a game at piquet, and I will play against you and my niece, for she must learn the game."

Tiretta asked leave of his darling to go to the play, and we played on till supper-time. On his return, Tiretta made us almost die of laughing with his attempts to tell us in his broken French the plot of the play he had seen.

I had been in my bedroom for a quarter of an hour, expecting to see my sweetheart in some pretty kind of undress, when all of a sudden I saw her come in with all her clothes on. I was surprised at this circumstance, and it seemed to me of evil omen.

"You are astonished to see me thus," said she, "but I want to speak to you for a moment, and then I will take off my clothes. Tell me plainly whether I am to consent to this marriage or no?"

"How do you like him?"

"Fairly well."

"Consent, then!"

"Very good; farewell! From this moment our love ends, and our friendship begins. Get you to bed, and I will go and do the same. Farewell!"

"No, stay, and let our friendship begin to-morrow."

"Not so, were my refusal to cost the lives of both of us. You know what it must cost me to speak thus, but it is my irrevocable determination. If I am to become another's wife, I must take care to be worthy of him; perhaps I may be happy. Do not hold me, let me go. You know how well I love you."

"At least, let us have one final embrace."

"Alas! no."

"You are weeping."

"No, I am not. In God's name let me go."

"Dear heart, you go but to weep in your chamber; stay here. I will marry you."

"Nay, no more of that."

With these words she made an effort, escaped from my hands, and fled from the room. I was covered with shame and regret, and could not sleep. I hated myself, for I knew not whether I had sinned most grievously in seducing her or in abandoning her to another.

I stayed to dinner next day in spite of my heartbreak and my sadness. Mdlle. de la Meure talked so brilliantly and sensibly to her intended that one could easily see he was enchanted with her. As for me, feeling that I had nothing pleasant to say, I pretended to have the toothache as an excuse for not talking. Sick at heart, absent-minded, and feeling the effects of a sleepless night, I was well-nigh mad with love, jealousy, and despair. Mdlle. de la Meure did not speak to me once, did not so much as look at me. She was quite right, but I did not think so then. I thought the dinner would never come to an end, and I do not think I was ever present at so painful a meal.

As we rose from the table, Madame went into her closet with her niece and nephew that was to be, and the niece came out in the course of an hour and bade us congratulate her, as she was to be married in a week, and after the wedding she would accompany her husband to Dunkirk. "To-morrow," she added, "we are all to dine with M. Corneman, where the deed of settlement will be signed."

I cannot imagine how it was I did not fall dead on the spot. My anguish cannot be expressed.

Before long it was proposed that we should go to the play, but excusing myself on the plea of business I returned to Paris. As I got to my door I seemed to be in a fever, and I lay down on my bed, but instead of the rest I needed I experienced only remorse and fruitless repentance-the torments of the damned. I began to think it was my duty to stop the marriage or die. I was sure that Mdlle. de la Meure loved me, and I fancied she would not say no if I told her that her refusal to marry me would cost me my life. Full of that idea I rose and wrote her a letter, strong with all the strength of tumultuous passion. This was some relief, and getting into bed I slept till morning. As soon as I was awake I summoned a messenger and promised him twelve francs if he would deliver my letter, and report its receipt in an hour and a half. My letter was under cover of a note addressed to Tiretta, in which I told him that I should not leave the house till I had got an answer. I had my answer four hours after; it ran as follows: "Dearest, it is too late; you have decided on my destiny, and I cannot go back from my word. Come to dinner at M. Corneman's, and be sure that in a few weeks we shall be congratulating ourselves on having won a great victory. Our love, crowned all too soon, will soon live only in our memories. I beg of you to write to me no more."

Such was my fate. Her refusal, with the still more cruel charge not to write to her again, made me furious. In it I only saw inconstancy. I thought she had fallen in love with the merchant. My state of mind may be judged from the fact that I determined to kill my rival. The most savage plans, the most cruel designs, ran a race through my bewildered brain. I was jealous, in love, a different being from my ordinary self; anger, vanity, and shame had destroyed my powers of reasoning. The charming girl whom I was forced to admire, whom I should have esteemed all the more for the course she had taken, whom I had regarded as an angel, became in my eyes a hateful monster, a meet object for punishment. At last I determined on a sure method of revenge, which I knew to be both dishonourable and cowardly, but in my blind passion I did not hesitate for a moment. I resolved to go to the merchant at M. Corneman's, where he was staying, to tell him all that had passed between the lady and myself, and if that did not make him renounce the idea of marrying her I would tell him that one of us must die, and if he refused my challenge I determined to assassinate him.

With this terrible plan in my brain, which makes me shudder now when I think of it, I ate with the appetite of a wild beast, lay down and slept till day. I was in the same mind when I awoke, and dressed myself hastily yet carefully, put two good pistols in my pocket and went to M. Corneman's. My rival was still asleep; I waited for him, and for a quarter of an hour my thoughts only grew more bitter and my determination more fixed. All at once he came into the room, in his dressing-gown, and received me with open arms, telling me in the kindest of voices that he had been expecting me to call, as he could guess what feelings I, a friend of his future wife's, could have for him, and saying that his friendship for me should always be as warm as hers. His honest open face, his straightforward words, overwhelmed me, and I was silent for a few minutes—in fact I did not know what to say. Luckily he gave me enough time to recollect myself, as he talked on for a quarter of an hour without noticing that I did not open my lips.

M. Corneman then came in; coffee was served, and my speech returned to me; but I am happy to say I refrained from playing the dishonourable part I had intended; the crisis was passed.

It may be remarked that the fiercest spirits are like a cord stretched too tight, which either breaks or relaxes. I have known several persons of that temperament—the Chevalier L——, amongst others, who in a fit of passion used to feel his soul escaping by every pore. If at the moment when his anger burst forth he was able to break something and make a great noise, he calmed down in a moment; reason resumed her sway, and the raging lion became as mild as a lamb.

After I had taken a cup of coffee, I felt myself calmed but yet dizzy in the head, so I bade them good morning and went out. I was astonished but delighted that I had not carried my detestable scheme into effect. I was humbled by being forced to confess to myself that chance and chance alone had saved me from becoming a villain. As I was reflecting on what had happened I met my brother, and he completed my cure. I took him to dine at Silvia's and stayed there till midnight. I saw that Mdlle. Baletti would make me forget the fair inconstant, whom I wisely determined not to see again before the wedding. To make sure I set out the next day for Versailles, to look after my interests with the Government.

CHAPTER II

*The Abby de la Ville—The Abby Galiani—The Neapolitan
Dialect—I Set Out for Dunkirk on a Secret Mission I Succeed—I
Return to Paris by Amiens—My Adventure by the Way—M. de
la Bretonniere—My Report Gives Satisfaction—I Am Paid Five
Hundred Louis—Reflections.*

A new career was opening before me. Fortune was still my friend,
and I had all the necessary qualities to second the efforts of the
blind goddess on my behalf save one—perseverance. My
immoderate life of pleasure annulled the effect of all my other
qualities.

M. de Bernis received me in his usual manner, that is more like a
friend than a minister. He asked me if I had any inclination for
a secret mission.

"Have I the necessary talents?"

"I think so."

"I have an inclination for all honest means of earning a livelihood,
and as for my talents I will take your excellency's opinion for
granted."

This last observation made him smile, as I had intended.

After a few words spoken at random on the memories of bygone
years which time had not entirely defaced, the minister told me to
go to the Abbe de la Ville and use his name.

This abbe, the chief permanent official of the foreign office, was a man of cold temperament, a profound diplomatist, and the soul of the department, and high in favour with his excellency the minister. He had served the state well as an agent at The Hague, and his grateful king rewarded him by giving him a bishopric on the day of his death. It was a little late, but kings have not always sufficient leisure to remember things. His heir was a wealthy man named Gamier, who had formerly been chief cook at M. d'Argenson's, and had become rich by profiting by the friendship the Abbe de la Ville had always had for him. These two friends, who were nearly of the same age, had deposited their wills in the hands of the same attorney, and each had made the other his residuary legatee.

After the abbe had delivered a brief discourse on the nature of secret missions and the discretion necessary to those charged with them, he told me that he would let me know when anything suitable for me presented itself.

I made the acquaintance of the Abbe Galiani, the secretary of the Neapolitan Embassy. He was a brother to the Marquis de Galiani, of whom I shall speak when we come to my Italian travels. The Abbe Galiani was a man of wit. He had a knack of making the most serious subjects appear comic; and being a good talker, speaking French with the ineradicable Neapolitan accent, he was a favourite in every circle he cared to enter. The Abbe de la Ville told him that Voltaire had complained that his Henriade had been translated into Neapolitan verse in such sort that it excited laughter.

"Voltaire is wrong," said Galiani, "for the Neapolitan dialect is of such a nature that it is impossible to write verses in it that are not laughable. And why should he be vexed; he who makes people laugh is sure of being beloved. The Neapolitan dialect is truly a singular one; we have it in translations of the Bible and of the Iliad, and both are comic."

"I can imagine that the Bible would be, but I should not have thought that would have been the case with the Iliad."

"It is, nevertheless."

I did not return to Paris till the day before the departure of Mdlle. de la Meure, now Madame P——. I felt in duty bound to go and see her, to give her my congratulations, and to wish her a pleasant journey. I found her in good spirits and quite at her ease, and, far from being vexed at this, I was pleased, a certain sign that I was cured. We talked without the slightest constraint, and I thought her husband a perfect gentleman. He invited us to visit him at Dunkirk, and I promised to go without intending to do so, but the fates willed otherwise.

Tiretta was now left alone with his darling, who grew more infatuated with her Strephon every day, so well did he prove his love for her.

With a mind at ease, I now set myself to sentimentalize with Mdlle. Baletti, who gave me every day some new mark of the progress I was making.

The friendship and respect I bore her family made the idea of seduction out of the question, but as I grew more and more in love with her, and had no thoughts of marriage, I should have been puzzled to say at what end I was aiming, so I let myself glide along the stream without thinking where I was going.

In the beginning of May the Abbe de Bernis told me to come and call on him at Versailles, but first to see the Abbe de la Ville. The first question the abbe asked me was whether I thought myself capable of paying a visit to eight or ten men-of-war in the roads at Dunkirk, of making the acquaintance of the officers, and of completing a minute and circumstantial report on the victualling, the number of seamen, the guns, ammunition, discipline, etc., etc.

"I will make the attempt," I said, "and will hand you in my report on my return, and it will be for you to say if I have succeeded or not."

"As this is a secret mission, I cannot give you a letter of commendation;
I can only give you some money and wish you a pleasant journey."

"I do not wish to be paid in advance—on my return you can give me what you think fit. I shall want three or four days before setting out, as I must procure some letters of introduction."

"Very good. Try to come back before the end of the month. I have no further instructions to give you."

On the same day I had some conversation at the Palais Bourbon with my patron, who could not admire sufficiently my delicacy in refusing payment in advance; and taking advantage of my having done so he made me accept a packet of a hundred Louis. This was the last occasion on which I made use of his purse; I did not borrow from him at Rome fourteen years afterwards.

"As you are on a secret mission, my dear Casanova, I cannot give you a passport. I am sorry for it, but if I did so your object would be suspected. However, you will easily be able to get one from the first gentleman of the chamber, on some pretext or other. Silvia will be more useful to you in that way than anybody else. You quite understand how discreet your behaviour must be. Above all, do not get into any trouble; for I suppose you know that, if anything happened to you, it would be of no use to talk of your mission. We should be obliged to know nothing about you, for ambassadors are the only avowed spies. Remember that you must be even more careful and reserved than they, and yet, if you wish to succeed, all this must be concealed, and you must have an air of freedom from constraint that you may inspire confidence. If, on your return, you like to shew me your report before handing it in, I will tell you what may require to be left out or added."

Full of this affair, the importance of which I exaggerated in proportion to my inexperience, I told Silvia that I wanted to accompany some English friends as far as Calais, and that she would oblige me by getting me a passport from the Duc de Gesvres. Always ready to oblige me, she sat down directly and wrote the duke a letter, telling me to deliver it myself since my personal description was necessary. These passports carry legal weight in the Isle de France only, but they procure one respect in all the northern parts of the kingdom.

Fortified with Silvia's letter, and accompanied by her husband, I went to the duke who was at his estate at St. Toro, and he had scarcely read the letter through before he gave me the passport. Satisfied on this point I went to Villette, and asked Madame if she had anything I could take to her niece. "You can take her the box of china statuettes," said she, "if M. Corneman has not sent them already." I called on the banker who gave me the box, and in return for a hundred Louis a letter of credit on a Dunkirk house. I begged him to name me in the letter in a special manner, as I was going for the sake of pleasure. He seemed glad to oblige me, and I started the same evening, and three days later I was at the "Hotel de la Conciergerie," in Dunkirk.

An hour after my arrival I gave the charming Madame P—— an agreeable surprise by handing her the box, and giving her her aunt's messages. Just as she was praising her husband, and telling me how happy she was, he came in, saying he was delighted to see me and asked me to stay in his house, without enquiring whether my stay in Dunkirk would be a long or short one. I of course thanked him, and after promising to dine now and again at his house I begged him to take me to the banker on whom I had a letter.

The banker read my letter, and gave me the hundred louis, and asked me to wait for him at my inn where he would come for me with the governor, a M. de Barail. This gentleman who, like most Frenchmen, was very polite, after making some ordinary enquiries, asked me to sup with him and his wife who was still at the play. The lady gave me as kind a reception as I had received from her husband. After we had partaken of an excellent supper several persons arrived, and play commenced in which I did not join, as I wished to study the society of the place, and above all certain officers of both services who were present. By means of speaking with an air of authority about naval matters, and by saying that I had served in the navy of the Venetian Republic, in three days I not only knew but was intimate with all the captains of the Dunkirk fleet. I talked at random about naval architecture, on the Venetian system of manoeuvres, and I noticed that the jolly sailors were better pleased at my blunders than at my sensible remarks.

Four days after I had been at Dunkirk, one of the captains asked me to dinner on his ship, and after that all the others did the same; and on every occasion I stayed in the ship for the rest of the day. I was curious about everything—and Jack is so trustful! I went into the hold, I asked questions innumerable, and I found plenty of young officers delighted to shew their own importance, who gossipped without needing any encouragement from me. I took care, however, to learn everything which would be of service to me, and in the evenings I put down on paper all the mental notes I had made during the day. Four or five hours was all I allowed myself for sleep, and in fifteen days I had learnt enough.

Pleasure, gaming, and idleness—my usual companions—had no part in this expedition, and I devoted all my energies to the object of my mission. I dined once with the banker, once with Madame P——, in the town, and once in a pretty country house which her husband had, at about a league's distance from Dunkirk. She took me there herself, and on finding myself alone with the woman I had loved so well I delighted her by the delicacy of my behaviour, which was marked only by respect and friendship. As I still thought her charming, and as our connection had only ended six weeks ago, I was astonished to see myself so quiet, knowing my disposition too well to attribute my restraint to virtue. What, then, was the reason? An Italian proverb, speaking for nature, gives the true solution of the riddle.

'La Mona non vuol pensieri', and my head was full of thought.

My task was done, and bidding good-bye to all my friends, I set out in my
post-chaise for Paris, going by another way for the sake of the change.
About midnight, on my asking for horses at some stage, the name of which
I forget, they told me that the next stage was the fortified town of Aire, which we should not be allowed to pass through at midnight.

"Get me the horses," said I, "I will make them open the gates."

I was obeyed, and in due time we reached the gates.

The postillion cracked his whip and the sentry called out, "Who goes there?"

"Express messenger."

After making me wait for an hour the gate was opened, and I was told that I must go and speak to the governor. I did so, fretting and fuming on my way as if I were some great person, and I was taken to a room where a man in an elegant nightcap was lying beside a very pretty woman.

"Whose messenger are you?"

"Nobody's, but as I am in a hurry."

"That will do. We will talk the matter over tomorrow. In the meanwhile you will accept the hospitality of the guard-room."

"But, sir . . ."

"But me no buts, if you please; leave the room."

I was taken to the guard-room where I spent the night seated on the ground. The daylight appeared. I shouted, swore, made all the racket I could, said I wanted to go on, but nobody took any notice of me.

Ten o'clock struck. More impatient than I can say, I raised my voice and spoke to the officer, telling him that the governor might assassinate me if he liked, but had no right to deny me pen and paper, or to deprive me of the power of sending a messenger to Paris.

"Your name, sir?"

"Here is my passport."

He told me that he would take it to the governor, but I snatched it away from him.

"Would you like to see the governor?"

"Yes, I should."

We started for the governor's apartments. The officer was the first to enter, and in two minutes came out again and brought me in. I gave up my passport in proud silence. The governor read it through, examining me all the while to see if I was the person described; he then gave it me back, telling me that I was free to go where I liked.

"Not so fast, sir, I am not in such a hurry now. I shall send a messenger to Paris and wait his return; for by stopping me on my journey you have violated all the rights of the subject."

"You violated them yourself in calling yourself a messenger."

"Not at all; I told you that I was not one."

"Yes, but you told your postillion that you were, and that comes to the same thing."

"The postillion is a liar, I told him nothing of the kind."

"Why didn't you shew your passport?"

"Why didn't you give me time to do so? In the course of the next few days we shall see who is right."

"Just as you please."

I went out with the officer who took me to the posting-place, and a minute afterwards my carriage drew up. The posting-place was also an inn, and I told the landlord to have a special messenger ready to carry out my orders, to give me a good room and a good bed, and to serve me some rich soup immediately; and I warned him that I was accustomed to good fare. I had my portmanteau and all my belongings taken into my room, and having washed and put on my dressing-gown I sat down to write, to whom I did not know, for I was quite wrong in my contention. However, I had begun by playing the great man, and I thought myself bound in honour to sustain the part, without thinking whether I stood to have to back out of it or no. All the same I was vexed at having to wait in Aire till the return of the messenger, whom I was about to send to the-moon! In the meanwhile, not having closed an eye all night, I determined to take a rest. I was sitting in my shirt-sleeves and eating the soup which had been served to me, when the governor came in unaccompanied. I was both surprised and delighted to see him.

"I am sorry for what has happened, sir, and above all that you think you have good reason for complaint, inasmuch as I only did my duty, for how was I to imagine that your postillion had called you a messenger on his own responsibility."

"That's all very well, sir, but your sense of duty need not have made you drive me from your room."

"I was in need of sleep."

"I am in the same position at the present moment, but a feeling of politeness prevents me from imitating your example."

"May I ask if you have ever been in the service?"

"I have served by land and sea, and have left off when most people are only beginning."

"In that case you will be aware that the gates of a fortified town are only opened by night to the king's messengers or to military superiors."

"Yes, I know; but since they were opened the thing was done, and you might as well have been polite."

"Will you not put on your clothes, and walk a short distance with me!"

His invitation pleased me as well as his pride had displeased me. I had been thinking of a duel as a possible solution of the difficulty, but the present course took all trouble out of my hands. I answered quietly and politely that the honour of walking with him would be enough to make me put off all other calls, and I asked him to be seated while I made haste to dress myself.

I drew on my breeches, throwing the splendid pistols in my pockets on to the bed, called up the barber, and in ten minutes was ready. I put on my sword, and we went out.

We walked silently enough along two or three streets, passed through a gate, up a court, till we got to a door where my guide stopped short. He asked me to come in, and I found myself in a fine room full of people. I did not think of going back, but behaved as if I had been in my own house.

"Sir-my wife," said the governor; and turning to her without pausing, "here is M. de Casanova, who has come to dinner with us."

"I am delighted to hear it, sir, as otherwise I should have had no chance of forgiving you for waking me up the other night."

"I paid dearly for my fault, madam, but after the purgatory I had endured
I am sure you will allow me to be happy in this paradise."

She answered with a charming smile, and after asking me to sit beside her she continued whatever conversation was possible in the midst of a game at cards.

I found myself completely outwitted, but the thing was done so pleasantly that all I could do was to put a good face on it—a feat which I found sufficiently easy from the relief I felt at no longer being bound to send a messenger to I did not know whom.

The governor well satisfied with his victory, got all at once into high spirits, and began to talk about military matters, the Court, and on general topics, often addressing me with that friendly ease which good French society knows so well how to reconcile with the rules of politeness; no one could have guessed that there had ever been the slightest difference between us. He had made himself the hero of the piece by the dexterous manner in which he had led up to the situation, but I had a fair claim to the second place, for I had made an experienced officer high in command give me the most flattering kind of satisfaction, which bore witness to the esteem with which I had inspired him.

The dinner was served. The success of my part depended on the manner in which it was played, and my wit has seldom been keener than during this meal. The whole conversation was in a pleasant vein, and I took great care to give the governor's wife opportunities for shining in it. She was a charming and pretty woman, still quite youthful, for she was at least thirty years younger than the governor. Nothing was said about my six hours' stay in the guard-room, but at dessert the governor escaped speaking plainly by a joke that was not worth the trouble of making.

"You're a nice man," said he, "to think I was going to fight you. Ah! ha!
I have caught you, haven't I?"

"Who told you that I was meditating a duel?"

"Confess that such was the case?"

"I protest; there is a great difference between believing and supposing; the one is positive, the other merely hypothetical. I must confess, however, that your invitation to take a walk roused my curiosity as to what was to come next, and I admire your wit. But you must believe me that I do not regard myself as caught in a trap—far from that, I am so well pleased that I feel grateful to you."

In the afternoon we all took a walk, and I gave my arm to the charming mistress of the house. In the evening I took my leave, and set out early the next day having made a fair copy of my report.

At five o'clock in the morning I was fast asleep in my carriage, when I was suddenly awakened. We were at the gate of Amiens. The fellow at the door was an exciseman—a race everywhere detested and with good cause, for besides the insolence of their manners nothing makes a man feel more like a slave than the inquisitorial search they are accustomed to make through one's clothes and most secret possessions. He asked me if I had anything contraband; and being in a bad temper at being deprived of my sleep to answer such a question I replied with an oath that I had nothing of the sort, and that he would have done better to let me sleep.

"As you talk in that style," said the creature, "we will see what we can see."

He ordered the postillion to pass on with the carriage. He had my luggage hauled down, and not being able to hinder him I fumed in silence.

I saw my mistake, but there was nothing to be done; and having no contraband goods I had nothing to fear, but my bad temper cost me two weary hours of delay. The joys of vengeance were depicted on the features of the exciseman. At the time of which I am writing these gaugers were the dregs of the people, but would become tractable on being treated with a little politeness. The sum of twenty-four sous given with good grace would make them as supple as a pair of gloves; they would bow to the travellers, wish them a pleasant journey, and give no trouble. I knew all this, but there are times when a man acts mechanically as I had done, unfortunately.

The scoundrels emptied my boxes and unfolded everything even to my shirts, between which they said I might have concealed English lace.

After searching everything they gave me back my keys, but they had not yet done with us; they began to search my carriage. The rascal who was at the head of them began to shout "victory," he had discovered the remainder of a pound of snuff which I had bought at St. Omer on my way to Dunkirk.

With a voice of triumph the chief exciseman gave orders that my carriage should be seized, and warned me that I would have to pay a fine of twelve hundred francs.

For the nonce my patience was exhausted, and I leave the names I called them to the imagination of the reader; but they were proof against words. I told them to take me to the superintendent's.

"You can go if you like," said they, "we are not your servants."

Surrounded by a curious crowd, whom the noise had drawn together, I began to walk hurriedly towards the town, and entering the first open shop I came to, I begged the shopkeeper to take me to the superintendent's. As I was telling the circumstances of the case, a man of good appearance, who happened to be in the shop, said that he would be glad to show me the way himself, though he did not think I should find the superintendent in, as he would doubtless be warned of my coming.

"Without your paying either the fine or caution money," said he, "you will find it a hard matter to get yourself out of the difficulty."

I entreated him to shew me the way to the superintendent's, and not to trouble about anything else. He advised me to give the rabble a louis to buy drink, and thus to rid myself of them, on which I gave him the louis, begging him to see to it himself, and the bargain was soon struck. He was a worthy attorney, and knew his men.

We got to the superintendent's; but, as my guide had warned me, my gentleman was not to be seen. The porter told us that he had gone out alone, that he would not be back before night, and that he did not know where he had gone.

"There's a whole day lost, then," said the attorney.

"Let us go and hunt him up; he must have well-known resorts and friends, and we will find them out. I will give you a louis for the day's work; will that be enough?"

"Ample."

We spent in vain four hours in looking for the superintendent in ten or twelve houses. I spoke to the masters of all of them, exaggerating considerably the injury that had been done to me. I was listened to, condoled with, and comforted with the remark that he would certainly be obliged to return to his house at night, and then he could not help hearing what I had to say. That would not suit me, so I continued the chase.

At one o'clock the attorney took me to an old lady, who was thought a great deal of in the town. She was dining all by herself. After giving great attention to my story, she said that she did not think she could be doing wrong in telling a stranger the whereabouts of an individual who, in virtue of his office, ought never to be inaccessible.

"And so, sir, I may reveal to you what after all is no secret. My daughter told me yesterday evening that she was going to dine at Madame N——'s, and that the superintendent was to be there. Do you go after him now, and you will find him at table in the best society in Amiens, but," said she, with a smile, "I advise you not to give your name at the door. The numerous servants will shew you the way without asking for your name. You can then speak to him whether he likes it or not, and though you don't know him he will hear all you say. I am sorry that I cannot be present at so fine a situation."

I gratefully took leave of the worthy lady, and I set off in all haste to the house I had been told of, the attorney, who was almost tired out, accompanying me. Without the least difficulty he and I slipped in between the crowds of servants till we got to a hall where there were more than twenty people sitting down to a rich and delicate repast.

"Ladies and gentlemen, you will excuse my troubling your quiet on this festive occasion with a tale of terror."

At these words, uttered in the voice of Jupiter Tonans, everybody rose. The surprise of the high-born company of knights and ladies at my apparition can easily be imagined.

"Since seven o'clock this morning I have been searching from door to door and from street to street for his honour the superintendent, whom I have at last been fortunate enough to find here, for I know perfectly well that he is present, and that if he have ears he hears me now. I am come to request him to order his scoundrelly myrmidons who have seized my carriage to give it up, so that I may continue my journey. If the laws bid me pay twelve hundred francs for seven ounces of snuff for my own private use, I renounce those laws and declare that I will not pay a farthing. I shall stay here and send a messenger to my ambassador, who will complain that the 'jus gentium' has been violated in the Ile-de-France in my person, and I will have reparation. Louis XV. is great enough to refuse to become an accomplice in this strange onslaught. And if that satisfaction which is my lawful right is not granted me, I will make the thing an affair of state, and my Republic will not revenge itself by assaulting Frenchmen for a few pinches of snuff, but will expel them all root and branch. If you want to know whom I am, read this."

Foaming with rage, I threw my passport on the table.

A man picked it up and read it, and I knew him to be the superintendent. While my papers were being handed round I saw expressed on every face surprise and indignation, but the superintendent replied haughtily that he was at Amiens to administer justice, and that I could not leave the town unless I paid the fine or gave surety.

"If you are here to do justice, you will look upon my passport as a positive command to speed me on my way, and I bid you yourself be my surety if you are a gentleman."

"Does high birth go bail for breaches of the law in your country?"

"In my country men of high birth do not condescend to take dishonourable employments."

"No service under the king can be dishonourable."

"The hangman would say the same thing."

"Take care what you say."

"Take care what you do. Know, sir, that I am a free man who has been grievously outraged, and know, too, that I fear no one. Throw me out of the window, if you dare."

"Sir," said a lady to me in the voice of the mistress of the house, "in my house there is no throwing out of windows."

"Madam, an angry man makes use of terms which his better reason disowns. I am wronged by a most cruel act of injustice, and I humbly crave your pardon for having offended you. Please to reflect that for the first time in my life I have been oppressed and insulted, and that in a kingdom where I thought myself safe from all but highway robbers. For them I have my pistols, and for the worthy superintendents I have a passport, but I find the latter useless. For the sake of seven ounces of snuff which I bought at St. Omer three weeks ago, this gentleman robs me and interrupts my journey, though the king's majesty is my surety that no one shall interfere with me; he calls on me to pay fifty louis, he delivers me to the rage of his impudent menials and to the derision of the mob, from whom I had to rid myself by my money and the aid of this worthy man beside me. I am treated like a scoundrel, and the man who should have been my defender and deliverer slinks away and hides himself, and adds to the insults I have received. His myrmidons have turned my clothes upside down, and pitchforked my linen at the foot of the town gates, to revenge themselves on me for not giving them twenty, four sous. To-morrow the manner in which I have been treated will be known to the diplomatic bodies at Versailles and Paris, and in a few days it will be in all the newspapers. I will pay not a farthing because I owe not a farthing. Now, sir, am I to send a courier to the Duc de Gesvres?"

"What you have got to do is to pay, and if you do not care to pay, you may do whatever you like."

"Then, ladies and gentlemen, good-bye. As for you, sir, we shall meet again."

As I was rushing out of the room like a madman, I heard somebody calling out to me in good Italian to wait a minute. I turned round, and saw the voice had proceeded from a man past middle age, who addressed the superintendent thus:—

"Let this gentleman proceed on his journey; I will go bail for him. Do you understand me, superintendent? I will be his surety. You don't know these Italians. I went through the whole of the last war in Italy, and I understand the national character. Besides, I think the gentleman is in the right."

"Very good," said the official, turning to me. "All you have to do is to pay a matter of thirty or forty francs at the customs' office as the affair is already booked."

"I thought I told you that I would not pay a single farthing, and I tell it you again. But who are you, sir," said I, turning to the worthy old man, "who are good enough to become surety for me without knowing me?"

"I am a commissary of musters, sir, and my name is de la Bretonnière. I live in Paris at the 'Hotel de Saxe,' Rue Colombien, where I shall be glad to see you after to-morrow. We will go together to M. Britard, who, after hearing your case, will discharge my bail."

After I had expressed my gratitude, and told him that I would wait upon him without fail, I made my excuses to the mistress of the house and the guests, and left them.

I took my worthy attorney to dinner at the best inn in the place, and I gave him two louis for his trouble. Without his help and that of the commissary I should have been in great difficulty; it would have been a case of the earthen pot and the iron pot over again; for with jacks-in-office reason is of no use, and though I had plenty of money I would never have let the wretches rob me of fifty louis.

My carriage was drawn up at the door of the tavern; and just as I was getting in, one of the excisemen who had searched my luggage came and told me that I should find everything just as I left it:—

"I wonder at that since it has been left in the hands of men of your stamp; shall I find the snuff?"

"The snuff has been confiscated, my lord."

"I am sorry for you, then; for if it had been there I would have given you a louis."

"I will go and look for it directly."

"I have no time to wait for it. Drive on, postillion."

I got to Paris the next day, and four days after I waited on M. de la Bretonnière, who gave me a hearty welcome, and took me to M. Britard, the fermier-general, who discharged his bail. This M. Britard was a pleasant young man. He blushed when he heard all I had gone through.

I took my report to M. de Bernis, at the "Hotel Bourbon," and his excellence spent two hours over it, making me take out all unnecessary matter. I spent the time in making a fair copy, and the next day I took it to M. de la Ville, who read it through in silence, and told me that he would let me know the result. A month after I received five hundred louis, and I had the pleasure of hearing that M. de Cremille, the first lord of the admiralty, had pronounced my report to be not only perfectly accurate but very suggestive. Certain reasonable apprehensions prevented me from making myself known to him—an honour which M. de Bernis wished to procure for me.

When I told him my adventures on the way back, he laughed, but said that the highest merit of a secret agent was to keep out of difficulties; for though he might have the tact to extricate himself from them, yet he got talked of, which it should be his chief care to avoid.

This mission cost the admiralty twelve thousand francs, and the minister might easily have procured all the information I gave him without spending a penny. Any intelligent young naval officer would have done it just as well, and would have acquitted himself with zeal and discretion, to gain the good opinion of the ministers. But all the French ministers are the same. They lavished money which came out of other people's pockets to enrich their creatures, and they were absolute; the downtrodden people counted for nothing, and of this course the indebtedness of the state and the confusion of the finances were the inevitable results. It is quite true that the Revolution was a necessity, but it should have been marked with patriotism and right feeling, not with blood. However, the nobility and clergy were not men of sufficient generosity to make the necessary sacrifices to the king, the state, and to themselves.

Silvia was much amused at my adventures at Aire and Amiens, and her charming daughter shewed much pity for the bad night I had passed in the guard-room. I told her that the hardship would have been much less if I had had a wife beside me. She replied that a wife, if a good one, would have been only too happy to alleviate my troubles by sharing in them, but her mother observed that a woman of parts, after seeing to the safety of my baggage and my coach, would have busied herself in taking the necessary steps for setting me at liberty, and I supported this opinion as best indicating the real duty of a good wife.

CHAPTER III

The Count de la Tour D'Auvergne and Madame D'Urfe—
Camille—My Passion for the Count's Mistress—The Ridiculous
Incident Which Cured Me—The Count de St. Germain

In spite of my love for Mdlle. Baletti, I did not omit to pay my
court to the most noted ladies of the pavement; but I was chiefly
interested in kept women, and those who consider themselves as
belonging to the public only in playing before them night by
night, queens or chamber-maids.

In spite of this affection, they enjoy what they call their
independence, either by devoting themselves to Cupid or to Plutus,
and more frequently to both together. As it is not very difficult to
make the acquaintance of these priestesses of pleasure and
dissipation, I soon got to know several of them.

The halls of the theatres are capital places for amateurs to exercise
their talents in intriguing, and I had profited tolerably well by the
lessons I had learnt in this fine school.

I began by becoming the friend of their lovers, and I often
succeeded by pretending to be a man of whom nobody need be
afraid.

Camille, an actress and dancer at the Italian play, with whom I
had fallen in love at Fontainebleu seven years ago, was one of
those of whom I was most fond, liking the society at her pretty
little house, where she lived with the Count d'Eigreville, who was a
friend of mine, and fond of my company. He was a brother of the

Marquis de Gamache and of the Countess du Rumain, and was a fine young fellow of an excellent disposition. He was never so well pleased as when he saw his mistress surrounded by people—a taste which is rarely found, but which is very convenient, and the sign of a temperament not afflicted by jealousy. Camille had no other lovers—an astonishing thing in an actress of the kind, but being full of tact and wit she drove none of her admirers to despair. She was neither over sparing nor over generous in the distribution of her favours, and knew how to make the whole town rave about her without fearing the results of indiscretion or sorrows of being abandoned.

The gentleman of whom, after her lover, she took most notice, was the Count de la Tour d'Auvergne, a nobleman of an old family, who idolized her, and, not being rich enough to possess her entirely, had to be content with what she gave him. Camille had given him a young girl, for whose keep she paid, who lived with Tour d'Auvergne in furnished apartments in the Rue de Taranne, and whom he said he loved as one loves a portrait, because she came from Camille. The count often took her with him to Camille's to supper. She was fifteen, simple in her manners, and quite devoid of ambition. She told her lover that she would never forgive him an act of infidelity except with Camille, to whom she felt bound to yield all since to her she owed all.

I became so much in love with her that I often went to Camille's solely to see her and to enjoy those artless speeches with which she delighted the company. I strove as best I could to conceal my flame, but often I found myself looking quite sad at the thought of the impossibility of my love being crowned with success. If I had let my passion be suspected I should have been laughed at, and should have made myself a mark for the pitiless sarcasms of Camille. However, I got my cure in the following ridiculous manner:—

Camille lived at the Barriere Blanche, and on leaving her house, one rainy evening, I sought in vain for a coach to take me home.

"My dear Casanova," said Tour d'Auvergne, "I can drop you at your own door without giving myself the slightest inconvenience, though my carriage is only seated for two; however, my sweetheart can sit on our knees."

I accepted his offer with pleasure, and we seated ourselves in the carriage, the count on my left hand and Babet on both our knees.

Burning with amorous passion I thought I would take the opportunity, and, to lose no time, as the coachman was driving fast, I took her hand and pressed it softly. The pressure was returned. Joy! I carried the hand to my lips, and covered it with affectionate though noiseless kisses. Longing to convince her of the ardour of my passion, and thinking that her hand would not refuse to do me a sweet service, I . . . but just at critical moment,

"I am really very much obliged to you, my dear fellow," said the Count de la Tour d'Auvergne, "for a piece of politeness thoroughly Italian, of which, however, I do not feel worthy; at least, I hope it's meant as politeness and not as a sign of contempt."

At these dreadful words I stretched out my hand and felt the sleeve of his coat. Presence of mind was no good in a situation like this, when his words were followed by a peal of loud laughter which would have confounded the hardiest spirit. As for me, I could neither join in his laughter nor deny his accusation; the situation was a fearful one, or would have been if the friendly shades of night had not covered my confusion. Babet did her best to find out from the count why he laughed so much, but he could not tell her for laughing, for which I gave thanks with all my heart. At last the carriage stopped at my house, and as soon as my servant had opened the door of my carriage I got down as fast as I could, and wished them good night—a compliment which Tour d'Auvergne returned with fresh peals of laughter. I entered my house in a state of stupefaction, and half an hour elapsed before I, too, began to laugh at the adventure. What vexed me most was the expectation of having malicious jests passed upon me, for I had not the least right to reckon on the count's discretion. However, I had enough sense to determine to join in the laughter if I could, and if not, to take it well, for this is, and always will be, the best way to get the laughers on one's own side at Paris.

For three days I saw nothing of the delightful count, and on the fourth I resolved to ask him to take breakfast with me, as Camille had sent to my house to enquire how I was. My adventure would not prevent me visiting her house, but I was anxious to know how it had been taken.

As soon as Tour d'Auvergne saw me he began to roar with laughter, and I joined in, and we greeted each other in the friendliest manner possible. "My dear count," said I, "let us forget this foolish story. You have no business to attack me, as I do not know how to defend myself."

"Why should you defend yourself, my dear fellow. We like you all the better for it, and this humorous adventure makes us merry every evening."

"Everybody knows it, then?"

"Of course, why not? It makes Camille choke with laughter. Come this evening; I will bring Babet, and she will amuse you as she maintains that you were not mistaken."

"She is right."

"Eh? what? You do me too much honour, and I don't believe you; but have it as you like."

"I can't do better, but I must confess when all's said that you were not the person to whom my fevered imagination offered such ardent homage."

At supper I jested, pretended to be astonished at the count's indiscretion, and boasted of being cured of my passion. Babet called me a villain, and maintained that I was far from cured; but she was wrong, as the incident had disgusted me with her, and had attached me to the count, who, indeed, was a man of the most amiable character. Nevertheless, our friendship might have been a fatal one, as the reader will see presently.

One evening, when I was at the Italian theatre, Tour d'Auvergne came up to me and asked me to lend him a hundred louis, promising to repay me next Saturday.

"I haven't got the money," I said, "but my purse and all it contains is at your service."

"I want a hundred louis, my dear fellow, and immediately, as I lost them at play yesterday evening at the Princess of Anhalt's."

"But I haven't got them."

"The receiver of the lottery ought always to be able to put his hand on a hundred louis."

"Yes, but I can't touch my cash-box; I have to give it up this day week."

"So you can; as I will repay you on Saturday. Take a hundred louis from the box, and put in my word of honour instead; don't you think that is worth a hundred Louis?"

"I have nothing to say to that, wait for me a minute."

I ran to my office, took out the money and gave it to him. Saturday came but no count, and as I had no money I pawned my diamond ring and replaced the hundred louis I owed the till. Three or four days afterwards, as I was at the Comedie Francaise, the Count de la Tour d'Auvergne came up to me and began to apologize. I replied by shewing my hand, and telling him that I had pawned my ring to save my honour. He said, with a melancholy air, that a man had failed to keep his word with him, but he would be sure to give me the hundred louis on the Saturday following, adding, "I give you my word of honour."

"Your word of honour is in my box, so let's say nothing about that. You can repay me when you like."

The count grew as pale as death.

"My word of honour, my dear Casanova, is more precious to me than my life; and I will give you the hundred louis at nine o'clock to-morrow morning at a hundred paces from the cafe at the end of the Champs-Elysees. I will give you them in person, and nobody will see us. I hope you will not fail to be there, and that you will bring your sword. I shall have mine."

"Faith, count! that's making me pay rather dear for my jest. You certainly do me a great honour, but I would rather beg your pardon, if that would prevent this troublesome affair from going any further."

"No, I am more to blame than you, and the blame can only be removed by the sword's point. Will you meet me?

"I do not see how I can refuse you, although I am very much averse to the affair."

I left him and went to Silvia's, and took my supper sadly, for I really liked this amiable nobleman, and in my opinion the game we were going to play was not worth the candle. I would not have fought if I could have convinced myself that I was in the wrong, but after turning the matter well-over, and looking at it from every point of view, I could not help seeing that the fault lay in the count's excessive touchiness, and I resolved to give him satisfaction. At all hazards I would not fail to keep the appointment.

I reached the cafe a moment after him. We took breakfast together and he payed. We then went out and walked towards the Etoile. When we got to a sheltered place he drew a bundle of a hundred louis from his pocket, gave it to me with the greatest courtesy, and said that one stroke of the sword would be sufficient. I could not reply.

He went off four paces and drew his sword. I did the same without saying a word, and stepping forward almost as soon as our blades crossed I thrust and hit him. I drew back my sword and summoned him to keep his word, feeling sure that I had wounded him in his chest.

He gently kissed his sword, and putting his hand into his breast he drew it out covered with blood, and said pleasantly to me, "I am satisfied."

I said to him all that I could, and all that it was my duty to say in the way of compliment, while he was stanching the blood with his handkerchief, and on looking at the point of my sword I was delighted to find that the wound was of the slightest. I told him so offering to see him home. He thanked me and begged me to keep my own counsel, and to reckon him henceforth amongst my truest friends. After I had embraced him, mingling my tears with my embraces, I returned home, sad at heart but having learnt a most useful lesson. No one ever knew of our meeting, and a week afterwards we supped together at Camille's.

A few days after, I received from M. de la Ville the five hundred louis for my Dunkirk mission. On my going to see Camille she told me that Tour d'Auvergne was kept in bed by an attack of sciatica, and that if I liked we could pay him a visit the next day. I agreed, and we went. After breakfast was over I told him in a serious voice that if he would give me a free hand I could cure him, as he was not suffering from sciatica but from a moist and windy humour which I could disperse my means of the Talisman of Solomon and five mystic words. He began to laugh, but told me to do what I liked.

"Very good, then I will go out and buy a brush."

"I will send a servant."

"No, I must get it myself, as I want some drugs as well." I bought some nitre, mercury, flower of sulphur, and a small brush, and on my return said, "I must have a little of your——, this liquid is indispensable, and it must be quite fresh."

Camille and he began to laugh, but I succeeded in keeping the serious face suitable to my office. I handed him a mug and modestly lowered the curtains, and he then did what I wanted.

I made a mixture of the various ingredients, and I told Camille that she must rub his thigh whilst I spoke the charm, but I warned her that if she laughed while she was about it it would spoil all. This threat only increased their good humour, and they laughed without cessation; for as soon as they thought they had got over it, they would look at one another, and after repressing themselves as long as they could would burst out afresh, till I began to think that I had bound them to an impossible condition. At last, after holding their sides for half an hour, they set themselves to be serious in real earnest, taking my imperturbable gravity for their example. De la Tour d'Auvergne was the first to regain a serious face, and he then offered Camille his thigh, and she, fancying herself on the boards, began to rub the sick man, whilst I mumbled in an undertone words which they would not have understood however clearly I had spoken, seeing that I did not understand them myself.

I was nearly spoiling the efficacy of the operation when I saw the grimaces they made in trying to keep serious. Nothing could be more amusing than the expression on Camille's face. At last I told her that she had rubbed enough, and dipping the brush into the mixture I drew on his thigh the five-pointed star called Solomon's seal. I then wrapped up the thigh in three napkins, and I told him that if he would keep quiet for twenty-four hours without taking off—his napkins, I would guarantee a cure.

The most amusing part of it all was, that by the time I had done the count and Camille laughed no more, their faces wore a bewildered look, and as for me . . . I could have sworn I had performed the most wonderful work in the world. If one tells a lie a sufficient number of times, one ends by believing it.

A few minutes after this operation, which I had performed as if by instinct and on the spur of the moment, Camille and I went away in a coach, and I told her so many wonderful tales that when she got out at her door she looked quite mazed.

Four or five days after, when I had almost forgotten the farce, I heard a carriage stopping at my door, and looking out of my window saw M. de la Tour d'Auvergne skipping nimbly out of the carriage.

"You were sure of success, then," said he, "as you did not come to see me the day after your astounding operation."

"Of course I was sure, but if I had not been too busy you would have seen me, for all that."

"May I take a bath?"

"No, don't bathe till you feel quite well."

"Very good. Everybody is in a state of astonishment at your feat, as I could not help telling the miracle to all my acquaintances. There are certainly some sceptics who laugh at me, but I let them talk."

"You should have kept your own counsel; you know what Paris is like.
Everybody will be considering me as a master-quack."

"Not at all, not at all. I have come to ask a favour of you."

"What's that?"

"I have an aunt who enjoys a great reputation for her skill in the occult sciences, especially in alchemy. She is a woman of wit, very, rich, and sole mistress of her fortune; in short, knowing her will do you no harm. She longs to see you, for she pretends to know you, and says that you are not what you seem. She has entreated me to take you to dine with her, and I hope you will accept the invitation. Her name is the Marchioness d'Urfe."

I did not know this lady, but the name of d'Urfe caught my attention directly, as I knew all about the famous Anne d'Urfe who flourished towards the end of the seventeenth century. The lady was the widow of his great-grandson, and on marrying into the family became a believer in the mystical doctrines of a science in which I was much interested, though I gave it little credit. I therefore replied that I should be glad to go, but on the condition that the party should not exceed the count, his aunt, and myself.

"She has twelve people every day to dinner, and you will find yourself in the company of the best society in Paris."

"My dear fellow, that's exactly what I don't want; for I hate to be thought a magician, which must have been the effect of the tales you have told."

"Oh, no! not at all; your character is well known, and you will find yourself in the society of people who have the greatest regard for you."

"Are you sure of that?"

"The Duchess de l'Oragnais told me, that, four or five years ago, you were often to be seen at the Palais Royal, and that you used to spend whole days with the Duchess d'Orleans; Madame de Bouffers, Madame de Blots, and Madame de Melfort have also talked to me about you. You are wrong not to keep up your old acquaintances. I know at least a hundred people of the first rank who are suffering from the same malady as that of which you cured me, and would give the half of their goods to be cured."

De la Tour d'Auvergne had reason on his side, but as I knew his wonderful cure had been due to a singular coincidence, I had no desire to expose myself to public ridicule. I therefore told him that I did not wish to become a public character, and that he must tell Madame d'Urfe that I would have the honour of calling on her in strict privacy only, and that she might tell me the day and hour on which I should kneel before her.

The same evening I had a letter from the count making an appointment at the Tuileries for the morrow; he was to meet me there, and take me to his aunt's to dinner. No one else was to be present.

The next day we met each other as had been arranged, and went to see Madame d'Urfe, who lived on the Quai des Theatins, on the same side as the "Hotel Bouillon."

Madame d'Urfe, a woman advanced in years, but still handsome, received me with all the courtly grace of the Court of the Regency. We spent an hour and a half in indifferent conversation, occupied in studying each other's character. Each was trying to get at the bottom of the other.

I had not much trouble in playing the part of the unenlightened, for such, in point of fact, was my state of mind, and Madame d'Urfe unconsciously betrayed the desire of shewing her learning;

this put me at my ease, for I felt sure I could make her pleased with me if I succeeded in making her pleased with herself.

At two o'clock the same dinner that was prepared every day for twelve was served for us three. Nothing worthy of note (so far as conversation went) was done at dinner, as we talked commonplace after the manner of people of fashion.

After the dessert Tour d'Auvergne left us to go and see the Prince de Turenne, who was in a high fever, and after he was gone Madame d'Urfe began to discuss alchemy and magic, and all the other branches of her beloved science, or rather infatuation. When we got on to the magnum opus, and I asked her if she knew the nature of the first matter, it was only her politeness which prevented her from laughing; but controlling herself, she replied graciously that she already possessed the philosopher's stone, and that she was acquainted with all the operations of the work. She then shewed me a collection of books which had belonged to the great d'Urfe, and Renee of Savoy, his wife; but she had added to it manuscripts which had cost her more than a hundred thousand francs. Paracelsus was her favourite author, and according to her he was neither man, woman, nor hermaphrodite, and had the misfortune to poison himself with an overdose of his panacea, or universal medicine. She shewed me a short manuscript in French, where the great work was clearly explained. She told me that she did not keep it under lock and key, because it was written in a cypher, the secret of which was known only to herself.

"You do not believe, then, in steganography."

"No, sir, and if you would like it, I will give you this which has been copied from the original."

"I accept it, madam, with all the more gratitude in that I know its worth."

From the library we went into the laboratory, at which I was truly astonished. She shewed me matter that had been in the furnace for fifteen years, and was to be there for four or five years more. It was a powder of projection which was to transform instantaneously all metals into the finest gold. She shewed me a pipe by which the coal descended to the furnace, keeping it always at the same heat. The lumps of coal were impelled by their own weight at proper intervals and in equal quantities, so that she was often three months without looking at the furnace, the temperature remaining the same the whole time. The cinders were removed by another pipe, most ingeniously contrived, which also answered the purpose of a ventilator.

The calcination of mercury was mere child's play to this wonderful woman. She shewed me the calcined matter, and said that whenever I liked she would instruct me as to the process. I next saw the Tree of Diana of the famous Taliamed, whose pupil she was. His real name was Maillot, and according to Madame d'Urfe he had not, as was supposed, died at Marseilles, but was still alive; "and," added she, with a slight smile, "I often get letters from him. If the Regent of France," said she, "had listened to me he would be alive now. He was my first friend; he gave me the name of Egeria, and he married me to M. d'Urfe."

She possessed a commentary on Raymond Lully, which cleared up all difficult points in the comments of Arnold de Villanova on the works of Roger Bacon and Heber, who, according to her, were still alive. This precious manuscript was in an ivory casket, the key of which she kept religiously; indeed her laboratory was a closed room to all but myself. I saw a small cask full of 'platina del Pinto', which she told me she could transmute into gold when she pleased. It had been given her by M. Vood himself in 1743. She shewed me the same metal in four phials. In the first three the platinum remained intact in sulphuric, nitric, and muriatic acid, but in the fourth, which contained 'aqua regia', the metal had not been able to resist the action of the acid. She melted it with the burning-glass, and said it could be melted in no other way, which proved, in her opinion, its superiority to gold. She shewed me some precipitated by sal ammoniac, which would not precipitate gold.

Her athanor had been alight for fifteen years. The top was full of black coal, which made me conclude that she had been in the laboratory two or three days before. Stopping before the Tree of Diana, I asked her, in a respectful voice, if she agreed with those who said it was only fit to amuse children. She replied, in a dignified manner, that she had made it to divert herself with the crystallization of the silver, spirit of nitre, and mercury, and that she looked upon it as a piece of metallic vegetation, representing in little what nature performed on a larger scale; but she added, very seriously, that she could make a Tree of Diana which should be a very Tree of the Sun, which would produce golden fruit, which might be gathered, and which would continue to be produced till no more remained of a certain ingredient. I said modestly that I could not believe the thing possible without the powder of projection, but her only answer was a pleased smile.

She then pointed out a china basin containing nitre, mercury, and sulphur, and a fixed salt on a plate.

"You know the ingredients, I suppose?" said she.

"Yes; this fixed salt is a salt of urine."

"You are right."

"I admire your sagacity, madam. You have made an analysis of the mixture with which I traced the pentacle on your nephew's thigh, but in what way can you discover the words which give the pentacle its efficacy?"

"In the manuscript of an adept, which I will shew you, and where you will find the very words you used."

I bowed my head in reply, and we left this curious laboratory.

We had scarcely arrived in her room before Madame d'Urfe drew from a handsome casket a little book, bound in black, which she put on the table while she searched for a match. While she was looking about, I opened the book behind her back, and found it to be full of pentacles, and by good luck found the pentacle I had traced on the count's thigh. It was surrounded by the names of the spirits of the planets, with the exception of those of Saturn and Mars. I shut up the book quickly. The spirits named were the same as those in the works of Agrippa, with which I was acquainted. With an unmoved countenance I drew near her, and she soon found the match, and her appearance surprised me a good deal; but I will speak of that another time.

The marchioness sat down on her sofa, and making me to do the like she asked me if I was acquainted with the talismans of the Count de Treves?

"I have never heard of them, madam, but I know those of Poliphilus:"

"It is said they are the same."

"I don't believe it."

"We shall see. If you will write the words you uttered, as you drew the pentacle on my nephew's thigh, and if I find the same talisman with the same words around it, the identity will be proved."

"It will, I confess. I will write the words immediately."

I wrote out the names of the spirits. Madame d'Urfe found the pentacle and read out the names, while I pretending astonishment, gave her the paper, and much to her delight she found the names to be the same.

"You see," said she, "that Poliphilus and the Count de Treves possessed the same art."

"I shall be convinced that it is so, if your book contains the manner of pronouncing the ineffable names. Do you know the theory of the planetary hours?"

"I think so, but they are not needed in this operation."

"They are indispensable, madam, for without them one cannot work with any certainty. I drew Solomon's pentacle on the thigh of Count de la Tour d'Auvergne in the hour of Venus, and if I had not begun with Arael, the spirit of Venus, the operation would have had no effect."

"I did not know that. And after Arael?"

"Next comes Mercury, then the Moon, then Jupiter, and then the Sun. It is, you see, the magic cycle of Zoroaster, in which Saturn and Mars are omitted."

"And how would you have proceeded if you had gone to work in the hour of the Moon?"

"I should have begun with Jupiter, passed to the Sun, then to Arael or
Venus, and I should have finished at Mercury."

"I see sir, that you are most apt in the calculation of the planetary hours."

"Without it one can do nothing in magic, as one would have no proper data; however, it is an easy matter to learn. Anyone could pick it up in a month's time. The practical use, however, is much more difficult than the theory; this, indeed, is a complicated affair. I never leave my house without ascertaining the exact number of minutes in the day, and take care that my watch is exact to the time, for a minute more or less would make all the difference in the world."

"Would you have the goodness to explain the theory to me."

"You will find it in Artephius and more clearly in Sandivogius."

"I have both works, but they are in Latin."

"I will make you a translation of them."

"You are very kind; I shall be extremely obliged to you."

"I have seen such things here, madam, that I could not refuse, for reasons which I may, perhaps, tell you to-morrow."

"Why not to-day?"

"Because I ought to know the name of your familiar spirit before I tell you."

"You know, then, that I have a familiar? You should have one, if it is true that you possess the powder of projection."

"I have one."

"Give me the oath of the order."

"I dare not, and you know why."

"Perhaps I shall be able to remove your fears by tomorrow."

This absurd oath was none other than that of the princes of the Rosy Cross, who never pronounce it without being certain that each party is a Rosicrucian, so Madame d'Urfe was quite right in her caution, and as for me I had to pretend to be afraid myself. The fact is I wanted to gain time, for I knew perfectly well the nature of the oath. It may be given between men without any indecency, but a woman like Madame d'Urfe would probably not relish giving it to a man whom she saw for the first time.

"When we find this oath alluded to in the Holy Scriptures," she said, "it is indicated by the words 'he swore to him by laying his hand on his thigh.'"

"But the thigh is not really what is meant; and consequently we never find any notice of a man taking this oath to a woman, as a woman has no 'verbum'."

The Count de la Tour d'Auvergne came back at nine o'clock in the evening, and he skewed no little astonishment at seeing me still with his aunt. He told us that his cousin's fever had increased, and that small-pox had declared itself; "and I am going to take leave of you, my dear aunt, at least for a month, as I intend to shut myself up with the sick man."

Madame d'Urfe praised his zeal, and gave him a little bag on his promising to return it to her after the cure of the prince.

"Hang it round his neck and the eruption will come out well, and he will be perfectly cured."

He promised to do so, and having wished us good evening he went out.

"I do not know, madam, what your bag contains, but if it have aught to do with magic, I have no confidence in its efficacy, as you have neglected to observe the planetary hour."

"It is an electrum, and magic and the observance of the hour have nothing to do with it."

"I beg your pardon."

She then said that she thought my desire for privacy praiseworthy, but she was sure I should not be ill pleased with her small circle, if I would but enter it.

"I will introduce you to all my friends," said she, "by asking them one at a time, and you will then be able to enjoy the company of them all."

I accepted her proposition.

In consequence of this arrangement I dined the next day with M. Grin and his niece, but neither of them took my fancy. The day after, I dined with an Irishman named Macartney, a physician of the old school, who bored me terribly. The next day the guest was a monk who talked literature, and spoke a thousand follies against Voltaire, whom I then much admired, and against the "Esprit des Lois," a favourite work of mine, which the cowled idiot refused to attribute to Montesquieu, maintaining it had been written by a monk. He might as well have said that a Capuchin created the heavens and the earth.

On the day following Madame d'Urfe asked me to dine with the Chevalier d'Arzigny, a man upwards of eighty, vain, foppish, and consequently ridiculous, known as "The Last of the Beaus." However, as he had moved in the court of Louis XIV., he was interesting enough, speaking with all the courtesy of the school, and having a fund of anecdote relating to the Court of that despotic and luxurious monarch.

His follies amused me greatly. He used rouge, his clothes were cut in the style which obtained in the days of Madame de Sevigne, he professed himself still the devoted lover of his mistress, with whom he supped every night in the company of his lady friends, who were all young and all delightful, and preferred his society to all others; however, in spite of these seductions, he remained faithful to his mistress.

The Chevalier d'Arzigny had an amiability of character which gave whatever he said an appearance of truth, although in his capacity of courtier truth was probably quite unknown to him. He always wore a bouquet of the most strongly-smelling flowers, such as tuberoses, jonquils, and Spanish jasmine; his wig was plastered down with amber-scented pomade, his teeth were made of ivory, and his eyebrows dyed and perfumed, and his whole person exhaled an odour to which Madame d'Urfe did not object, but which I could scarcely bear. If it had not been for this drawback I should probably have cultivated his society. He was a professed Epicurean, and carried out the system with an amazing tranquillity. He said that he would undertake to receive twenty-four blows with the stick every morning on the condition that he should not die within the twenty-four hours, and that the older he grew the more blows he would gladly submit to. This was being in love with life with a vengeance.

Another day I dined with M. Charon, who was a counsellor, and in charge of a suit between Madame d'Urfe and her daughter

Madame du Chatelet, whom she disliked heartily. The old counsellor had been the favoured lover of the marchioness forty years before, and he thought himself bound by the remembrance of their love-passages to support the cause of his old sweetheart. In those days French magistrates thought they had a right to take the side of their friends, or of persons in whom they had an interest, sometimes for friendship's sake, and sometimes for a monetary consideration; they thought, in fact, that they were justified in selling justice.

M. Charon bored me like the others, as was natural, considering we had no two tastes in common.

The scene was changed the next day when I was amused with the company of M. de Viarme, a young counsellor, a nephew of Madame d'Urfe's, and his pretty and charming wife. He was the author of the "Remonstrances to the King," a work which got him a great reputation, and had been read eagerly by the whole town. He told me that the business of a counsellor was to oppose everything done by the crown, good and bad. His reasons for this theory were those given by all minorities, and I do not think I need trouble my readers with them.

The most enjoyable dinner I had was with Madame de Gergi, who came with the famous adventurer, known by the name of the Count de St. Germain. This individual, instead of eating, talked from the beginning of the meal to the end, and I followed his example in one respect as I did not eat, but listened to him with the greatest attention. It may safely be said that as a conversationalist he was unequalled.

St. Germain gave himself out for a marvel and always aimed at exciting amazement, which he often succeeded in doing. He was scholar, linguist, musician, and chemist, good-looking, and a perfect ladies' man. For awhile he gave them paints and cosmetics; he flattered them, not that he would make them young again (which he modestly confessed was beyond him) but that their beauty would be preserved by means of a wash which, he said, cost him a lot of money, but which he gave away freely.

He had contrived to gain the favour of Madame de Pompadour, who had spoken about him to the king, for whom he had made a laboratory, in which the monarch—a martyr to boredom—tried to find a little pleasure or distraction, at all events, by making dyes. The king had given him a suite of rooms at Chambord, and a hundred thousand francs for the construction of a laboratory, and according to St. Germain the dyes discovered by the king would have a materially beneficial influence on the quality of French fabrics.

This extraordinary man, intended by nature to be the king of impostors and quacks, would say in an easy, assured manner that he was three hundred years old, that he knew the secret of the Universal Medicine, that he possessed a mastery over nature, that he could melt diamonds, professing himself capable of forming, out of ten or twelve small diamonds, one large one of the finest water without any loss of weight. All this, he said, was a mere trifle to him. Notwithstanding his boastings, his bare-faced lies, and his manifold eccentricities, I cannot say I thought him offensive. In spite of my knowledge of what he was and in spite of my own feelings, I thought him an astonishing man as he was always astonishing me. I shall have something more to say of this character further on.

When Madame d'Urfe had introduced me to all her friends, I told her that I would dine with her whenever she wished, but that with the exception of her relations and St. Germain, whose wild talk amused me, I should prefer her to invite no company. St. Germain often dined with the best society in the capital, but he never ate anything, saying that he was kept alive by mysterious food known only to himself. One soon got used to his eccentricities, but not to his wonderful flow of words which made him the soul of whatever company he was in.

By this time I had fathomed all the depths of Madame d'Urfe's character. She firmly believed me to be an adept of the first order, making use of another name for purposes of my own; and five or six weeks later she was confirmed in this wild idea on her asking me if I had diciphered the manuscript which pretended to explain the Magnum Opus.

"Yes," said I, "I have deciphered it, and consequently read it, and I now beg to return it you with my word of honour that I have not made a copy; in fact, I found nothing in it that I did not know before."

"Without the key you mean, but of course you could never find out that."

"Shall I tell you the key?"

"Pray do so."

I gave her the word, which belonged to no language that I know of, and the marchioness was quite thunderstruck.

"This is too amazing," said she; "I thought myself the sole possessor of that mysterious word—for I had never written it down, laying it up in my memory—and I am sure I have never told anyone of it."

I might have informed her that the calculation which enabled me to decipher the manuscript furnished me also with the key, but the whim took me to tell her that a spirit had revealed it to me. This foolish tale completed my mastery over this truly learned and sensible woman on everything but her hobby. This false confidence gave me an immense ascendancy over Madame d'Urfe, and I often abused my power over her. Now that I am no longer the victim of those illusions which pursued me throughout my life, I blush at the remembrance of my conduct, and the penance I impose on myself is to tell the whole truth, and to extenuate nothing in these Memoirs.

The wildest notion in the good marchioness's brain was a firm belief in the possibility of communication between mortals and elementary spirits. She would have given all her goods to attain to such communication, and she had several times been deceived by impostors who made her believe that she attained her aim.

"I did not think," said she, sadly, "that your spirit would have been able to force mine to reveal my secrets."

"There was no need to force your spirit, madam, as mine knows all things of his own power."

"Does he know the inmost secrets of my soul?"

"Certainly, and if I ask him he is forced to disclose all to me."

"Can you ask him when you like?"

"Oh, yes! provided I have paper and ink. I can even ask him questions through you by telling you his name."

"And will you tell it me?"

"I can do what I say; and, to convince you, his name is Paralis. Ask him a simple question in writing, as you would ask a common mortal. Ask him, for instance, how I deciphered your manuscript, and you shall see I will compel him to answer you."

Trembling with joy, Madame d'Urfe put her question, expressed it in numbers, then following my method in pyramid shape; and I made her extract the answer, which she wrote down in letters. At first she only obtained consonants, but by a second process which supplied the vowels she received a clear and sufficient answer. Her every feature expressed astonishment, for she had drawn from the pyramid the word which was the key to her manuscript. I left her, carrying with me her heart, her soul, her mind, and all the common sense which she had left.

CHAPTER IV

Absurd Ideas of Madame D'Urfe on My Supernatural Powers—Marriage of My Brother—I Conceive a Plan on His Wedding Day—I Go to Holland on a Financial Mission—The Jew Boaz Gives Me a Lesson—M. d'Afri—Esther—Another Casanova—I Find Therese Imer Again

By the time that the Prince du Turenne had recovered from the small-pox and the Count de la Tour d'Auvergne had left him, the latter, knowing his aunt's taste for the occult sciences, was not surprised to find me become her confident and most intimate friend.

I was glad so see him and all the relations of the marchioness at dinner, as I was delighted with the courtesy with which they treated me. I am referring more especially to her brothers MM. de Pont-Carre and de Viarme who had lately been chosen head of the trade companies, and his son. I have already spoken of Madame du Chatelet, the marchioness's daughter, but an unlucky lawsuit separated them, and she no longer formed one of the family circle.

De la Tour d'Auvergne having been obliged to rejoin his regiment which was in garrison in Brittany, the marchioness and I dined together almost every day and people looked upon me as her husband, and despite the improbability of the supposition this was the only way in which they could account for the long hours we spent together. Madame d'Urfe thought that I was rich and looked upon my position at the lottery as a mere device for preserving my incognito.

I was the possessor in her estimation, not only of the philosopher's stone, but also of the power of speaking with the whole host of elementary spirits; from which premises she drew the very logical deduction that I could turn the world upside down if I liked, and be the blessing or the plague of France; and she thought my object in remaining incognito was to guard myself from arrest and imprisonment; which according to her would be the inevitable result of the minister's discovering my real character. These wild notions were the fruit of the nocturnal revelations of her genius, that is, of the dreams of her disordered spirit, which seemed to her realities. She did not seem to think that if I was endowed as she supposed no one would have been able to arrest me, in the first place, because I should have had foreknowledge of the attempt, and in the second place because my power would have been too strong for all bolts and bars. All this was clear enough, but strong passion and prejudice cannot reason.

One day, in the course of conversation, she said, with the utmost seriousness, that her genius had advised her that not even I had power to give her speech with the spirits, since she was a woman, and the genii only communicated with men, whose nature is more perfect. Nevertheless, by a process which was well known to me, I might make her soul pass into the body of a male child born of the mystic connection between a mortal and an immortal, or, in other words, between an ordinary man and a woman of a divine nature.

If I had thought it possible to lead back Madame d'Urfe to the right use of her senses I would have made the attempt, but I felt sure that her disease was without remedy, and the only course before me seemed to abet her in her ravings and to profit by them.

If I had spoken out like an honest man and told her that her theories were nonsensical, she would not have believed me; she would have thought me jealous of her knowledge, and I should have lost her favour without any gain to her or to myself. I thus let things take their course, and to speak the truth I was flattered to see myself treated as one of the most profound brothers of the Rosy Cross, as the most powerful of men by so distinguished a lady, who was in high repute for her learning, who entertained and was related to the first families of France, and had an income of eighty thousand francs, a splendid estate, and several magnificent houses in Paris. I was quite sure that she would refuse me nothing, and though I had no definite plan of profiting by her wealth I experienced a certain pleasure at the thought that I could do so if I would.

In spite of her immense fortune and her belief in her ability to make gold, Madame d'Urfe was miserly in her habits, for she never spent more than thirty thousand francs in a year, and she invested her savings in the exchange, and in this way had nearly doubled them. A brother used to buy her in Government securities at their lowest rate and sell at their rise, and in this manner, being able to wait for their rise, and fall, she had amassed a considerable sum.

She had told me more than once that she would give all she possessed to become a man, and that she knew I could do this for her if I would. One day, as she was speaking to me on this subject in a tone of persuasion almost irresistible, I told her that I must confess I had the power to do what she wanted, but that I could not make up my mind to perform the operation upon her as I should have to kill her first. I thought this would effectually check her wish to go any further, but what was my surprise to hear her say,

"I know that, and what is more I know the death I shall have to die; but for all that I am ready."

"What, then, is that death, madam?"

"It is by the same poison which killed Paracelsus."

"Do you think that Paracelsus obtained the hypostasis?"

"No, but I know the reason of his not doing so."

"What is the reason?"

"It is that he was neither man or woman, and a composite nature is incapable of the hypostasis, to obtain which one must be either the one or the other."

"Very true, but do you know how to make the poison, and that the thing is impossible without the aid of a salamander?"

"That may or may not be! I beseech you to enquire of the oracle whether there be anyone in Paris in possession of this potion."

It was easy to see that she thought herself in possession of it, so I had no hesitation in extracting her name from the oracular pyramid. I pretended to be astonished at the answer, but she said boastfully,

"You see that all we want is a male child born of an immortal. This, I am advised, will be provided by you; and I do not think you will be found wanting out of a foolish pity for this poor old body of mine."

At these words I rose and went to the window, where I stayed for more than a quarter of an hour reflecting on her infatuation. When I returned to the table where she was seated she scanned my features attentively, and said, with much emotion, "Can it be done, my dear friend? I see that you have been weeping."

I did not try to undeceive her, and, taking my sword and hat, I took leave of her sadly. Her carriage, which was always at my disposal, was at the door, and I drove to the Boulevards, where I walked till the evening, wondering all the while at the extraordinary fantasies of the marchioness.

My brother had been made a member of the Academy, on the exhibition of a battle piece which had taken all the critics by storm. The picture was purchased by the Academy for five hundred louis.

He had fallen in love with Caroline, and would have married her but for a piece of infidelity on her part, which so enraged him that in a week after he married an Italian dancer. M. de Sanci, the ecclesiastical commissioner, gave the wedding party. He was fond of the girl, and out of gratitude to my brother for marrying her he got him numerous orders among his friends, which paved the way to the large fortune and high repute which my brother afterwards attained.

M. Corneman, the banker, who was at my brother's wedding, spoke to me at considerable length on the great dearth of money, and asked me to discuss the matter with the comptroller-general.

He told me that one might dispose of Government securities to an association of brokers at Amsterdam, and take in exchange the securities of any other country whose credit was higher than that of France, and that these securities could easily be realized. I begged him to say no more about it, and promised to see what I could do.

The plan pleased me, and I turned it over all night; and the next day I went to the Palais Bourbon to discuss the question with M. de Bernis. He thought the whole idea an excellent one, and advised me to go to Holland with a letter from M. de Choiseul for M. d'Afri, the ambassador at the Hague. He thought that the first person I should consult with M. de Boulogne, with whom he warned me to appear as if I was sure of my ground.

"As you do not require money in advance," said he, "you will be able to get as many letters of recommendation as you like."

The same day I went to the comptroller-general, who approved of my plan, and told me that M. le Duc de Choiseul would be at the Invalides the next day, and that I should speak to him at once, and take a letter he would write for me.

"For my part," said he, "I will credit our ambassador with twenty millions, and if, contrary to my hopes, you do not succeed, the paper can be sent back to France."

I answered that there would be no question of the paper being returned, if they would be content with a fair price.

"The margin will be a small one; however, you will hear about that from the ambassador, who will have full instructions."

I felt so flattered by this mission that I passed the night in thinking it over. The next day I went to the Invalides, and M. de Choiseul, so famous for taking decisive action, had no sooner read M. de Boulogne's letter and spoken a few words to me on the subject, than he got me to write a letter for M. d'Afri, which he signed, sealed, returned to me, and wished me a prosperous journey.

I immediately got a passport from M. de Berkenrode, and the same day took leave of Madame Baletti and all my friends except Madame d'Urfe, with whom I was to spend the whole of the next day. I gave my clerk at the lottery office full authority to sign all tickets.

About a month before, a girl from Brussels, as excellent as she was pretty, had been married under my auspices to an Italian named Gaetan, by trade a broker. This fellow, in his fit of jealousy, used to ill-treat her shamefully; I had reconciled them several times already, and they regarded me as a kind of go-between. They came to see me on the day on which I was making my preparations for going to Holland. My brother and Tiretta were with me, and as I was still living in furnished apartments I took them all to Laudel's, where they gave one an excellent dinner.

Tiretta, drove his coach-and-four; he was ruining his ex-methodist, who was still desperately in love with him.

In the course of dinner Tiretta, who was always in high spirits and loved a jest, began to flirt with the girl, whom he saw for the first time. She, who neither meant nor suspected any ill, was quite at her ease, and we should have enjoyed the joke, and everything would have gone on pleasantly, if her husband had possessed some modicum of manners and common sense, but he began to get into a perfect fury of jealousy. He ate nothing, changed colour ten times in a minute, and looked daggers at his wife, as much as to say he did not see the joke. To crown all, Tiretta began to crack jests at the poor wretch's expense, and I, foreseeing unpleasantness, endeavoured, though all in vain, to moderate his high spirits and his sallies. An oyster chanced to fall on Madame Gaetan's beautiful breast; and Tiretta, who was sitting near her, took it up with his lips as quick as lightning. Gaetan was mad with rage and gave his wife such a furious box on the ear that his hand passed on from her cheek to that of her neighbour. Tiretta now as enraged as Gaetan took him by his middle and threw him down, where, having no arms, he defended himself with kicks and fisticuffs, till the waiter came, and we put him out of the room.

The poor wife in tears, and, like Tiretta, bleeding at the nose, besought me to take her away somewhere, as she feared her husband would kill her if she returned to him. So, leaving Tiretta with my brother, I got into a carriage with her and I took her, according to her request, to her kinsman, an old attorney who lived in the fourth story of a house in the Quai de Gevres. He received us politely, and after having heard the tale, he said,

"I am a poor man, and I can do nothing for this unfortunate girl; while if I had a hundred crowns I could do everything."

"Don't let that stand in your way," said I, and drawing three hundred francs from my pockets I gave him the money.

"Now, sir," said he, "I will be the ruin of her husband, who shall never know where his wife is."

She thanked me and I left her there; the reader shall hear what became of her when I return from my journey.

On my informing Madame d'Urfe that I was going to Holland for the good of France, and that I should be coming back at the beginning of February, she begged me to take charge of some shares of hers and to sell them for her. They amounted in value to sixty thousand francs, but she could not dispose of them on the Paris Exchange owing to the tightness in the money market. In addition, she could not obtain the interest due to her, which had mounted up considerably, as she had not had a dividend for three years.

I agreed to sell the shares for her, but it was necessary for me to be constituted depositary and owner of the property by a deed, which was executed the same day before a notary, to whose office we both went.

On returning to her house I wished to give her an I O U for the moneys, but she would not hear of such a thing, and I let her remain satisfied of my honesty.

I called on M. Corneman who gave me a bill of exchange for three hundred florins on M. Boaz, a Jewish banker at the Hague, and I then set out on my journey. I reached Anvers in two days, and finding a yacht ready to start I got on board and arrived at Rotterdam the next day. I got to the Hague on the day following, and after depositing my effects at the "Hotel d'Angleterre" I proceeded to M. d'Afri's, and found him reading M. de Choiseul's letter, which informed him of my business. He asked me to dine in his company and in that of the ambassador of the King of Poland, who encouraged me to proceed in my undertaking though he had not much opinion of my chances of success.

Leaving the ambassador I went to see Boaz, whom I found at table in the midst of a numerous and ugly family. He read my letter and told me he had just received a letter from M. Corneman in which I was highly commended to him. By way of a joke he said that as it was Christmas Eve he supposed I should be going to rock the infant Jesus asleep, but I answered that I was come to keep the Feast of the Maccabees with him—a reply which gained me the applause of the whole family and an invitation to stay with them. I accepted the offer without hesitation, and I told my servant to fetch my baggage from the hotel. Before leaving the banker I asked him to shew me some way of making twenty thousand florins in the short time I was going to stay in Holland.

Taking me quite seriously he replied that the thing might easily be done and that he would think it over.

The next morning after breakfast, Boaz said,

"I have solved your problem, sir; come in here and I will tell you about it."

He took me into his private office, and, after counting out three thousand florins in notes and gold, he told me that if I liked I could undoubtedly make the twenty thousand florins I had spoken of.

Much surprised at the ease with which money may be got in Holland, as I had been merely jesting in the remarks I had made, I thanked him for his kindness, and listened to his explanation.

"Look at this note," said he, "which I received this morning from the Mint. It informs me that an issue of four hundred thousand ducats is about to be made which will be disposed of at the current rate of gold, which is fortunately not high just now. Each ducat will fetch five florins, two stivers and three-fifths. This is the rate of exchange with Frankfort. Buy in four hundred thousand ducats; take them or send them to Frankfort, with bills of exchange on Amsterdam, and your business is done. On every ducat you will make a stiver and one-ninth, which comes to twenty-two thousand, two hundred and twenty-two of our florins. Get hold of the gold to-day, and in a week you will have your clear profit. That's my idea."

"But," said I, "will the clerks of the Mint trust me with such a sum?"

"Certainly not, unless you pay them in current money or in good paper."

"My dear sir, I have neither money nor credit to that amount."

"Then you will certainly never make twenty thousand florins in a week. By the way you talked yesterday I took you for a millionaire."

"I am very sorry you were so mistaken."

"I shall get one of my sons to transact the business to-day."

After giving me this rather sharp lesson, M. Boaz went into his office, and I went to dress.

M. d'Afri had paid his call on me at the "Hotel d'Angleterre," and not finding me there he had written me a letter asking me to come and see him. I did so, and he kept me to dinner, shewing me a letter he had received from M. de Boulogne, in which he was instructed not to let me dispose of the twenty millions at a greater loss than eight per cent., as peace was imminent. We both of us laughed at this calm confidence of the Parisian minister, while we who were in a country where people saw deeper into affairs knew that the truth was quite otherwise.

On M. d'Afri's hearing that I was staying with a Jew, he advised me to keep my own counsel when with Jews, "because," said he, "in business, most honest and least knavish mean pretty much the same thing. If you like," he added, "I will give you a letter of introduction to M. Pels, of Amsterdam." I accepted his offer with gratitude, and in the hope of being useful to me in the matter of my foreign shares he introduced me to the Swedish ambassador, who sent me to M. d'O——.

Wanting to be present at a great festival of Freemasons on St. John's Day, I remained at the Hague till the day after the celebration. The Comte de Tot, brother of the baron, who lost all his money at the seraglio, and whom I had met again at the Hague, introduced me. I was not sorry to be in company with all the best society in Holland.

M. d'Afri introduced me to the mother of the stadtholder, who was only twelve, and whom I thought too grave for his years. His mother was a worthy, patient kind of woman, who fell asleep every minute, even while she was speaking. She died shortly after, and it was discovered at the postmortem examination that she had a disease of the brain which caused her extreme propensity to sleep. Beside her I saw Count Philip de Zinzendorf, who was looking for twelve millions for the empress—a task which was not very difficult, as he offered five per cent. interest.

At the play I found myself sitting next to the Turkish minister, and I thought he would die with laughter before my eyes. It happened thus:

They were playing Iphigenia, that masterpiece of Racine's. The statue of Diana stood in the midst of the stage, and at the end of one act Iphigenia and her train of priestesses, while passing before it, all made a profound bow to the goddess. The candlesnuffer, who perhaps may have been a bad wit, crossed the stage just after wards, and likewise bowed to the goddess. This put pit and boxes in a good humour, and peals of laughter sounded from all parts of the house. All this had to be explained to the Turk, and he fell into such a fit of laughter that I thought he would burst. At last he was carried to his inn still laughing but almost senseless.

To have taken no notice of the Dutchman's heavy wit would have been, I confess, a mark of stupidity, but no one but a Turk could have laughed like that. It may be said that a great Greek philosopher died of laughter at seeing a toothless old woman trying to eat figs. But there is a great difference between a Turk and a Greek, especially an ancient Greek.

Those who laugh a good deal are more fortunate than those who do not laugh at all, as laughter is good for the digestion; but there is a just mean in everything.

When I had gone two leagues from Amsterdam in my posting-chaise on two wheels, my servant sitting beside me, I met a carriage on four wheels, drawn like mine by two horses, and containing a fine-looking young man and his servant. His coachman called out to mine to make way for him. My coachman answered that if he did he might turn me into the ditch, but the other insisted on it. I spoke to the master, begging him to tell his coachman to make way for me.

"I am posting, sir," said I; "and, moreover, I am a foreigner."

"Sir," answered he, "in Holland we take no notice of posting or not posting; and if you are foreigner, as you say, you must confess that you have fewer rights than I who am in my own country."

The blood rushed to my face. I flung open the door with one hand and took my sword with the other; and leaping into the snow, which was up to my knees, I drew my sword, and summoned the Dutchman to give way or defend himself. He was cooler than I, and replied, smiling, that he was not going to fight for so foolish a cause, and that I might get into my carriage again, as he would make way for me. I was somewhat interested in his cool but pleasant manner. I got back into my chaise, and the next night reached Amsterdam.

I put up at the excellent inn "L'Etoile d'Orient," and in the morning I went on 'Change and found M. Pels. He told me he would think my business over, and finding M, d'O—— directly afterwards he offered to do me my sixty bills and give me twelve per cent. M. Pels told me to wait, as he said he could get me fifteen per cent. He asked me to dinner, and, on my admiring his Cape wine, he told me with a laugh that he had made it himself by mixing Bordeaux and Malaga.

M. d'O—— asked me to dinner on the day following; and on calling I found him with his daughter Esther, a young lady of fourteen, well developed for her age, and exquisite in all respects except her teeth, which were somewhat irregular. M. d'O was a widower, and had this only child; consequently, Esther was heiress to a large fortune. Her excellent father loved her blindly, and she deserved his love. Her skin was snow white, delicately tinted with red; her hair was black as ebony, and she had the most beautiful eyes I have ever seen. She made an impression on me. Her father had given her an excellent education; she spoke French perfectly, played the piano admirably, and was passionately fond of reading.

After dinner M. d'O—— shewed me the uninhabited part of the house, for since the death of his wife, whose memory was dear to him, he lived on the ground floor only. He shewed me a set of rooms where he kept a treasure in the way of old pottery. The walls and windows were covered with plates of marble, each room a different colour, and the floors were of mosaic, with Persian carpets. The dining-hall was cased in alabaster, and the table and the cupboards were of cedar wood. The whole house looked like a block of solid marble, for it was covered with marble without as well as within, and must have cost immense sums. Every Saturday half-a-dozen servant girls, perched on ladders, washed down these splendid walls. These girls wore wide hoops, being obliged to put on breeches, as otherwise they would have interested the passers by in an unseemly manner. After looking at the house we went down again, and M. d'O—— left me alone with Esther in the antechamber, where he worked with his clerks. As it was New Year's Day there was not business going on.

After playing a sonata, Mdlle. d'O—— asked me if I would go to a concert. I replied that, being in her company, nothing could make me stir. "But would you, mademoiselle, like to go?"

"Yes, I should like to go very well, but I cannot go by myself."

"If I might presume to offer to escort you . . . but I dare not think you would accept."

"I should be delighted, and if you were to ask my father I am sure he would not refuse his permission."

"Are you sure of that?"

"Quite sure, for otherwise he would be guilty of impoliteness, and my father would not do such a thing. But I see you don't know the manners of the country."

"I confess I do not:"

"Young ladies enjoy great liberty here—liberty which they lose only by marrying. Go and ask, and you will see:"

I went to M. d'O—— and made my request, trembling lest I should meet with a refusal.

"Have you a carriage?"

"Yes, sir."

"Then I need not give orders to get mine ready. Esther!"

"Yes, father."

"Go and dress, my dear; M. Casanova has been kind enough to offer to take you to the concert."

"How good of him! Thank you, papa, for letting me go."

She threw her arms around his neck, ran to dress, and reappeared an hour after, as fair as the joy which was expressed on her every feature. I could have wished she had used a little powder, but Esther was jealous of her ebon tresses, which displayed the whiteness of her skin to admiration. The chief aim of women in making their toilette is to please men, but how poor is the judgment of most men in such matters compared to the unerring instinct of the generality of women!

A beautiful lace kerchief veiled her bosom, whose glories made my heart beat faster.

We went down the stair, I helped her into the carriage, and stopped, thinking she would be accompanied by one of her women; but seeing nobody I got in myself. The door was shut, and we were off. I was overwhelmed with astonishment. A treasure like this in my keeping I could hardly think. I asked myself whether I was to remember that I was a free-lance of love, or whether honour bade me forget it. Esther, in the highest spirits, told me that we were going to hear an Italian singer whose voice was exquisite, and noticing my confusion she asked what was the matter. I did not know what to say, and began to stammer out something, but at last succeeded in saying that she was a treasure of whom I was not worthy to be the keeper.

"I know that in other countries a young girl would not be trusted alone with a gentleman, but here they teach us discretion and how to look after ourselves."

"Happy the man who is charged with your welfare, and happier still he on whom your choice has fallen!"

"That choice is not for me to make; 'tis my father's business."

"But supposing your father's choice is not pleasing to you, or supposing you love another?"

"We are not allowed to love a man until we know he is to be our husband."

"Then you are not in love with anyone?"

"No, and I have never felt the desire to love."

"Then I may kiss your hand?"

"Why should you kiss my hand?"

She drew away her hand and offered me her lovely lips. I took a kiss, which she gave modestly enough, but which went to my heart. My delight was a little alloyed when she said that she would give me another kiss before her father whenever I liked.

We reached the concert-room, where Esther found many of her young friends—all daughters of rich merchants, some pretty, some plain, and all curious to know who I was. The fair Esther, who knew no more than my name, could not satisfy them. All at once seeing a fair young girl a little way off she pointed her out to me and asked me my opinion of her. Naturally enough I replied that I did not care for fair girls.

"All the same, I must introduce you to her, for she may be a relation of yours. Her name is the same; that is her father over there:"

"M. Casanova," said she, speaking to a gentleman, "I beg to introduce to you M. Casanova, a friend of my father's."

"Really? The same name; I wish, sir, you were my friend, as we are, perhaps, related. I belong to the Naples branch."

"Then we are related, though distantly, as my father came from Parma.
Have you your pedigree?"

"I ought to have such a thing, but to tell you the truth, I don't think much of such matters. Besants d'or and such heraldic moneys are not currency in a mercantile republic."

"Pedigree-hunting is certainly a somewhat foolish pursuit; but it may nevertheless afford us a few minutes' amusement without our making any parade of our ancestry."

"With all my heart."

"I shall have the honour of calling on you to-morrow, and I will bring my family-tree with me. Will you be vexed if you find the root of your family also?"

"Not at all; I shall be delighted. I will call on you myself to-morrow.
May I ask if you are a business man?"

"No, I am a financial agent in the employ of the French ministry. I am staying with M. Pels."

M. Casanova made a sign to his daughter and introduced me to her. She was Esther's dearest friend, and I sat down between them, and the concert began.

After a fine symphony, a concerto for the violin, another for the hautbois, the Italian singer whose repute was so great and who was styled Madame Trend made her appearance. What was my surprise when I recognized in her Therese Imer, wife of the dancer Pompeati, whose name the reader may remember. I had made her acquaintance eighteen years ago, when the old senator Malipiero had struck me because we were playing together. I had seen her again at Venice in 1753, and then our pastime had been of a more serious nature. She had gone to Bayreuth, where she had been the margrave's mistress. I had promised to go and see her, but C——C—— and my fair nun M—— M—— had left me neither the time nor the wish to do so. Soon after I was put under the Leads, and then I had other things to think about. I was sufficiently self-controlled not to shew my astonishment, and listened to an aria which she was singing, with her exquisite voice, beginning "Eccoti giunta al fin, donna infelice," words which seemed made for the case.

The applause seemed as if it would never come to an end. Esther told me that it was not known who she was, but that she was said to be a woman with a history, and to be very badly off. "She goes from one town to another, singing at all the public concerts, and all she receives is what those present choose to give her on a plate which she takes round."

"Does she find that pay?"

"I should suspect not, as everyone has paid already at coming in. She cannot get more than thirty or forty florins. The day after to-morrow she will go to the Hague, then to Rotterdam, then back here again. She had been performing for six months, and she is always well received."

"Has she a lover?"

"She is said to have lovers in every town, but instead of enriching her they make her poorer. She always wears black, not only because she is a widow, but also on account of a great grief she is reported to have gone through. She will soon be coming round." I took out my purse; and counted out twelve ducats, which I wrapped in paper; my heart beating all the while in a ridiculous manner, for I had really nothing to be excited about.

When Therese was going along the seats in front of me, I glanced at her for an instant, and I saw that she looked surprised. I turned my head to speak to Esther, and when she was directly in front of me I put my little packet on the plate without looking at her, and she passed on. A little girl, four or five years old, followed her, and when she got to the end of the bench she came back to kiss my hand. I could not help recognizing in her a facsimile of myself, but I concealed my emotion. The child stood still, and gazed at me fixedly, to my no small confusion. "Would you like some sweets, my dear?" said I, giving her my box, which I should have been glad to turn into gold. The little girl took it smilingly, made me a curtsy, and went on.

"Does it strike you, M. Casanova," said Esther, with a laugh, "that you and that little girl are as like each other as two peas?"

"Yes, indeed," added Mdlle. Casanova, "there is a striking likeness."

"These resemblances are often the work of chance."

"Just so," said Esther, with a wicked smile, "but you admit a likeness, don't you?"

"I confess I was struck with it, though of course I cannot judge so well as you."

After the concert M. d'O—— arrived, and giving back his daughter to his care I betook myself to my lodging. I was just sitting down to a dish of oysters, before going to bed, when Therese made her appearance, holding her child by the hand. Although I had not expected her to visit me that evening, I was nevertheless not much surprised to see her. I, of course, rose to greet her, when all at once she fell fainting on the sofa, though whether the fainting fit was real or assumed I cannot say. Thinking that she might be really ill I played my part properly, and brought her to herself by sprinkling her with cold water and putting my vinaigrette to her nose. As soon as she came to herself she began to gaze at me without saying a word. At last, tired of her silence, I asked her if she would take any supper; and on her replying in the affirmative, I rang the bell and ordered a good supper for three, which kept us at the table till seven o'clock in the morning, talking over our various fortunes and misfortunes. She was already acquainted with most of my recent adventures, but I knew nothing at all about hers, and she entertained me with a recital of them for five or six hours.

Sophie, the little girl, slept in my bed till day, and her mother, keeping the best of her tale to the last, told me that she was my daughter, and shewed me her baptismal certificate. The birth of the child fell in with the period at which I had been intimate with Therese, and her perfect likeness to myself left no room for doubt. I therefore raised no objections, but told the mother that I was persuaded of my paternity, and that, being in a position to give the child a good education, I was ready to be a father to her.

"She is too precious a treasure in my sight; if we were separated I should die."

"You are wrong; for if I took charge of the little girl I should see that she was well provided for."

"I have a son of twelve to whom I cannot give a proper education; take charge of him instead of Sophie."

"Where is he?"

"He is boarding, or rather in pawn, at Rotterdam."

"What do you mean by in pawn?"

"I mean that he will not be returned to me until I pay the person who has got him all my debts."

"How much do you owe?"

"Eighty florins. You have already given me sixty-two, give me four ducats more; you can then take my son, and I shall be the happiest of mothers. I will send my son to you at the Hague next week, as I think you will be there."

"Yes, my dear Therese; and instead of four ducats, here are twenty."

"We shall see each other again at the Hague."

She was grateful to excess, but I only felt pity for her and a sort of friendly interest, and kept quite cool, despite the ardour of her embraces. Seeing that her trouble was of no avail, she sighed, shed some tears, and, taking her daughter, she bid me adieu, promising once more to send me her son.

Therese was two years older than I. She was still pretty, and even handsome, but her charms no longer retained their first beauty, and my passion for her, having been a merely physical one, it was no wonder that she had no longer any attraction for me. Her adventures during the six years in which I had lost her would certainly interest my readers, and form a pleasing episode in my book, and I would tell the tale if it were a true one; but not being a romance writer, I am anxious that this work shall contain the truth and nothing but the truth. Convicted by her amorous and jealous margrave of infidelity, she had been sent about her business. She was separated from her husband Pompeati, had followed a new lover to Brussels, and there had caught the fancy of Prince Charles de Lorraine, who had obtained her the direction of all the theatres in the Austrian Low Countries. She had then undertaken this vast responsibility, entailing heavy expenditure, till at last, after selling all her diamonds and lace, she had fled to Holland to avoid arrest. Her husband killed himself at Vienna in a paroxysm caused by internal pain—he had cut open his stomach with a razor, and died tearing at his entrails.

My business left me no time for sleep. M. Casanova came and asked me to dinner, telling me to meet him on the Exchange—a place well worth seeing. Millionaires are as plentiful as blackberries, and anyone who is not worth more than a hundred thousand florins is considered a poor man. I found M. d'O—— there, and was asked by him to dinner the following day at a small house he had on the Amstel. M. Casanova treated me with the greatest courtesy. After reading my pedigree he went for his own, and found it exactly the same; but he merely laughed, and seemed to care little about it, differing in that respect from Don Antonio of Naples, who set such store by my pedigree, and treated me with such politeness on that account. Nevertheless, he bade me make use of him in anything relating to business if I did anything in that way. I thought his daughter pretty, but neither her charms nor her wit made any impression on me. My thoughts were taken up with Esther, and I talked so much about her at dinner that at last my cousin declared that she did not consider her pretty. Oh, you women! beauty is the only unpardonable offence in your eyes. Mdlle. Casanova was Esther's friend, and yet she could not bear to hear her praised.

On my seeing M. d'O—— again after dinner, he told me that if I cared to take fifteen per cent. on my shares, he would take them from me and save broker's expenses. I thought the offer a good one, and I accepted it, taking a bill of exchange on Tourton & Baur. At the rate of exchange at Hamburg I found I should have seventy-two thousand francs, although at five per cent. I had only expected sixty-nine thousand. This transaction won me high favour with Madame d'Urfe, who, perhaps, had not expected me to be so honest.

In the evening I went with M. Pels to Zaandam, in a boat placed on a sleigh and impelled by a sail. It was an extraordinary, but at the same time an amusing and agreeable, mode of travelling. The wind was strong, and we did fifteen miles an hour; we seemed to pass through the air as swiftly as an arrow. A safer and more convenient method of travelling cannot be imagined; it would be an ideal way of journeying round the world if there were such a thing as a frozen sea all round. The wind, however, must be behind, as one cannot sail on a side wind, there being no rudder. I was pleased and astonished at the skill of our two sailors in lowering sail exactly at the proper time; for the sleigh ran a good way, from the impetus it had already received, and we stopped just at the bank of the river, whereas if the sail had been lowered a moment later the sleigh might have been broken to pieces. We had some excellent perch for dinner, but the strength of the wind prevented us from walking about. I went there again, but as Zaandam is well known as the haunt of the millionaire merchants who retire and enjoy life there in their own way, I will say no more about it. We returned in a fine sleigh drawn by two horses, belonging to M. Pels, and he kept me to supper. This worthy man, whose face bore witness to his entire honesty, told me that as I was now the friend of M. d'O—— and himself, I should have nothing whatever to do with the Jews, but should address myself to them alone. I was pleased with this proposal, which made a good many of my difficulties disappear, and the reader will see the results of this course.

Next day snow fell in large flakes, and I went early to M. d'O——'s, where I found Esther in the highest of spirits. She gave me a warm welcome, and began to rally me on having spent the whole night with Madame Trenti.

I might possibly have shewn some slight confusion, but her father said an honest man had nothing to be ashamed of in admiring talent. Then, turning to me, he said,

"Tell me, M. Casanova, who this woman is?"

"She is a Venetian whose husband died recently; I knew her when I was a lad, and it was six years since I had seen her last."

"You were agreeably surprised, then, to see your daughter?" said Esther.

"Why do you think the child is my daughter? Madame Trenti was married then."

"The likeness is really too strong. And how about your falling asleep yesterday when you were supping with M. Pels?"

"It was no wonder that I went asleep, as I had not closed an eye the night before."

"I am envious of anyone who possesses the secret of getting a good sleep, for I have always to wait long hours before sleep comes to me, and when I awake, instead of being refreshed, I feel heavy and languid from fatigue."

"Try passing the night in listening to one in whom you take an interest, telling the story of her life, and I promise you that you will sleep well the night after."

"There is no such person for me."

"No, because you have as yet only seen fourteen summers; but afterwards there will be someone."

"Maybe, but what I want just now is books, and the help of someone who will guide my reading."

"That would be an easy matter for anyone who knew your tastes."

"I like history and travels, but for a book to please me it must be all true, as I lay it down at the slightest suspicion of its veracity."

"Now I think I may venture to offer my services, and if you will accept them I believe I shall be able to give satisfaction."

"I accept your offer, and shall keep you to your word."

"You need not be afraid of my breaking it, and before I leave for the
Hague I will prove that I am reliable."

She then began to rally me on the pleasure I should have at the Hague, where I should see Madame Trenti again. Her freedom,

mirth, and extreme beauty set my blood on fire, and M. d'O——
laughed heartily at the war his charming daughter waged on me.
At eleven o'clock we got into a well-appointed sleigh and we set out
for his small house, where she told me I should find Mdlle.
Casanova and her betrothed.

"Nevertheless," said I, "you will continue to be my only attraction."

She made no answer, but it was easy to perceive that my avowal
had not displeased her.

When we had gone some distance we saw the lovers, who had come
out, in spite of the snow, to meet us. We got down, and after
taking off our furs we entered the house. I gazed at the young
gentleman, who looked at me a moment in return and then
whispered in Mdlle. Casanova's ear. She smiled and whispered
something to Esther. Esther stepped up to her father and said a few
words to him in a low voice, and everybody began to laugh at
once. They all looked at me and I felt certain that I was somehow
the point of the joke, but I put on an indifferent air.

"There may be a mistake," said M. d'O——; "at any rate we should
ascertain the truth of the matter."

"M. Casanova, had you any adventures on your journey from the
Hague to
Amsterdam?"

At this I looked again at the young gentleman, and I guessed
what they were talking about.

"No adventure to speak of," I answered, "except a meeting with a fine fellow who desired to see my carriage turn upside down into the ditch, and who I think is present now."

At these words the laughter broke out afresh, and the gentleman and I embraced each other; but after he had given the true account of the adventure his mistress pretended to be angry, and told him that he ought to have fought. Esther observed that he had shewn more true courage in listening to reason, and M. d'O—— said he was strongly of his daughter's opinion; however, Mdlle. Casanova, after airing her high-flown ideas, began to sulk with her lover.

To restore the general mirth, Esther said, gaily, "Come, come, let us put on our skates, and try the Amstel, for I am afraid that unless we go forthwith the ice will have melted." I was ashamed to ask her to let me off, though I would gladly have done so! but what will not love do! M. d'O—— left us to our own devices. Mdlle. Casanova's intended put on my skates, and the ladies put on their short petticoats with black velvet drawers to guard against certain accidents. We reached the river, and as I was a perfect neophyte in this sport the figure I cut may be imagined. However, I resolutely determined to conquer my awkwardness, and twenty times, to the peril of my spine, did I fall down upon the ice. I should have been wiser to have left off, but I was ashamed to do so, and I did not stop till, to my huge delight, we were summoned in to dinner. But I paid dear for my obstinacy, for when I tried to rise from the table I felt as if I had lost the use of my limbs. Esther pitied me, and said she would cure me. There was a good deal of laughter at my expense, and I let them laugh, as I felt certain that the whole thing had been contrived to turn me into derision, and wishing to make Esther love me I thought it best to stimulate a good temper. I passed the afternoon with M. d'O——, letting the young people go by themselves on the Amstel, where they stopped till dusk.

Next morning when I awoke I thought I was a lost man. I suffered a martyrdom of pain. The last of my vertebral bones, called by doctors the os sacrum, felt as if it had been crushed to atoms, although I had used almost the whole of a pot of ointment which Esther had given me for that purpose. In spite of my torments I did not forget my promise, and I had myself taken to a bookseller's where I bought all the books I thought likely to interest her. She was very grateful, and told me to come and embrace her before I started if I wanted a pretty present.

It was not likely that I was going to refuse such an invitation as that, so I went early in the morning, leaving my post-chaise at the door Her governess took me to her bed, where she was lying as fair and gay as Venus herself.

"I am quite sure," said she, "that you would not have come at all unless
I had asked you to come and embrace me."

At this my lips were fastened on her mouth, her eyes, and on every spot of her lovely face. But seeing my eyes straying towards her bosom, and guessing that I should make myself master of it, she stopped laughing and put herself on the defensive.

"Go away," said she, slyly, "go away and enjoy yourself at the Hague with the fair Trenti, who possesses so pretty a token of your love."

"My dear Esther, I am going to the Hague to talk business with the ambassador, and for no other reason, and in six days at latest you will see me back again, as much your lover as before, and desiring nothing better than to please you."

"I rely upon your word of honour, but mind you do not deceive me."

With these words she put up her mouth and gave me so tender and passionate a kiss that I went away feeling certain of my bliss being crowned on my return. That evening, at supper-time, I reached Boaz's house.

The End